T0323587

Cambridge Elements

Elements in Religion and Monotheism
edited by
Paul K. Moser
Loyola University Chicago
Chad Meister
*Affiliate Scholar, Ansari Institute for Global Engagement with Religion,
University of Notre Dame*

MONOTHEISM
AND RELATIVISM

Bernd Irlenborn
Faculty of Theology, Paderborn (Germany)

CAMBRIDGE
UNIVERSITY PRESS

Shaftesbury Road, Cambridge CB2 8EA, United Kingdom

One Liberty Plaza, 20th Floor, New York, NY 10006, USA

477 Williamstown Road, Port Melbourne, VIC 3207, Australia

314–321, 3rd Floor, Plot 3, Splendor Forum, Jasola District Centre, New Delhi – 110025, India

103 Penang Road, #05–06/07, Visioncrest Commercial, Singapore 238467

Cambridge University Press is part of Cambridge University Press & Assessment, a department of the University of Cambridge.

We share the University's mission to contribute to society through the pursuit of education, learning and research at the highest international levels of excellence.

www.cambridge.org
Information on this title: www.cambridge.org/9781009571937

DOI: 10.1017/9781009376211

First published 2025

A catalogue record for this publication is available from the British Library

ISBN 978-1-009-57193-7 Hardback
ISBN 978-1-009-37619-8 Paperback
ISSN 2631-3014 (online)
ISSN 2631-3006 (print)

Monotheism and Relativism

Elements in Religion and Monotheism

DOI: 10.1017/9781009376211
First published online: January 2025

Bernd Irlenborn
Faculty of Theology, Paderborn (Germany)

Author for correspondence: Bernd Irlenborn, b.irlenborn@thf-paderborn.de

Abstract: This Element explores the relationship between monotheism and relativism. Over the last two decades, emerging relativist theories have been extensively developed and debated within the fields of philosophy. How does monotheistic theology relate to relativism, especially to relativism about truth? Given that truth relativism contends that beliefs and propositions are only relatively true, it appears to conflict with traditional monotheism, which asserts the absolute truth of God's existence. This Element examines the compatibility of relativist positions with monotheism, emphasising the need to differentiate among the diverse forms, types, and domains of relativism. It presents a nuanced stance on the relationship between relativism and monotheism.

Keywords: relativism, monotheism, truth, revelation, absolutism

ISBNs: 9781009571937 (HB), 9781009376198 (PB), 9781009376211 (OC)
ISSNs: 2631-3014 (online), 2631-3006 (print)

Contents

1 Introduction

This Cambridge Element explores the relationship between monotheism and relativism. Several key themes are to be considered: What is meant by the concept of relativism? Does it refer to a uniform idea or a variety of different notions and approaches? What are the core ideas in monotheism? Which monotheistic religions need to be examined for our topic? How do the doctrines of relativism and monotheism relate? Are they somehow compatible, or does monotheism in certain ways exclude, or even contradict, relativism? Alternatively, should we assume other structures for their relationship? Or, should we be cautious, given that the question of how such comprehensive theories relate might already be too general?

With regard to relativism, emerging relativist theories have gained considerable importance over the last two decades. These conceptions of relativism have been developed across a range of fields, including metaphysics, semantics, epistemology, logic, the philosophy of science, ethics, and also the philosophy of religion and monotheistic theology. However, the proliferation of relativist ideas, concepts, and theories has led to increasingly polarised debates in some areas between the defenders and detractors of relativism. While the latter often view relativism as an incoherent position or, more strongly, as a philosophical disease of modernity, the former defend it as a project promoting tolerance and understanding in the face of global plurality and diversity of cultures, beliefs, and claims to truth. Roughly speaking, relativism revolves around the idea that something is relative to something else. More precisely, the general idea of relativism holds that X (a statement, proposition, belief, norm, value, etc.) is not true objectively or does not apply absolutely (independent of time, place, perspective, etc.), but is only true relatively, depending on a particular parameter Y (a worldview, cognitive scheme, context, culture, conceptual framework, language, etc.). Consider the following assertions as examples: 'Meaning is relative to a particular language', 'Human rights are relative to the Western moral code', 'Beauty is relative to a standard of taste', and 'Religious beliefs are relative to a particular culture'.

As we will explore in more detail in Section 2, there are not only different fields or domains in which versions of relativism aim to resolve specific philosophical problems (such as epistemic, moral, and conceptual relativism), but there are also various forms of relativism that are categorised as global or local, weak or strong, or normative or descriptive. Furthermore, it is possible to be a relativist in terms of a particular version of relativism and, at the same time, an absolutist – the opposite of a relativist – in terms of another version of relativism. Within the different versions of relativism, truth or alethic relativism (from *alēthēs*, the Greek word for 'true') holds central significance. Broadly speaking, it encompasses the idea that the truth (or falsity) of statements is not absolute but relative, depending upon specific parameters, such as the culture, context, or tradition in which they are accepted. Truth relativism is implicit in the wide range of relativist statements asserting that an X is relative to a Y, as these assertions typically claim to be true in a relative sense. For instance, epistemic relativism can be described as the claim that the truth of beliefs about justification is relative to certain cognitive parameters, whereas moral relativism may be viewed as the claim that the truth of beliefs about moral values is relative to certain moral frameworks. In this respect, relativist claims of this type are reducible to truth relativism (Baghramian 2004: 121). Notably, relativists are generally not opposed to the idea of truth itself but rather to an absolute conception of it.

At this point, our topic 'Monotheism and Relativism' becomes relevant. What is monotheism, and how is it linked to relativism? Wide and narrow concepts of monotheism exist. In general, traditional monotheism asserts that a single and supreme deity or divine being purposefully created the world and continues to interact with it in various ways (for example, through different forms of self-revelation), while remaining supernatural and transcendent. Within the monotheistic religions of Judaism, Christianity, and Islam, this supreme being is most commonly referred to as 'God', an infinite agent exhibiting all the cognitive qualities humans possess (such as self-awareness and rationality), but without any limitations. More specifically, traditional monotheism posits the existence of a singular, supreme, and all-good God who created the world and continues to intervene in it, such that the evolutionary history of life over extended periods has led to the emergence of human beings as the primary recipients of his divine affection. Correspondingly, human destiny is to respond to the Creator's grace and affection through faith, worship, and good deeds, in the hope of redemption from sin and the attainment of eternal life with him.

As omnipotent, omniscient, and omnibenevolent, God alone is deemed worthy of worship. He is revered as the founder of all creation, the embodiment of truth itself, or, in the words of the Bible, 'the way, and the truth, and the life' (John 14:6).[1] Derived from this understanding of God's existence as an absolute fact, independent of the human mind, monotheistic beliefs about God and his creation usually assume – mostly based on divine revelation and within the limits of human knowledge – that claims about the metaphysical nature of the world are objectively true. The underlying rationale is that a belief about

---

[1] Biblical quotations are taken from the New Revised Standard Version.

the world is true in an absolute or objective sense if what it claims is indeed the case, independent of our epistemic ability to ultimately conceive or verify it.[2] Thus, the monotheistic assertion 'There is a supreme, transcendent God' is true if this supreme, transcendent God really exists, regardless of our knowledge about him. In this regard, monotheists generally maintain that this assertion is not relatively true, namely, only for believers or dependent on a particular religious worldview, but objectively or absolutely, meaning it is true in all places, at all times, and for all people.

How does monotheism relate to relativism, especially to relativism about truth? Insofar as strong alethic relativism is committed to the view that no objective truths exist – since statements, beliefs, or propositions are invariably only relatively true – it seems to be at variance with traditional monotheism and its adherence to the absolute truth of God's existence. For instance, within the framework of alethic relativism, the assertion that one supreme God exists, if considered relatively true, could be true only for those who believe, and not for everyone, as the objective perspective would assert. Accordingly, monotheism would be one of many different, relatively true and equally legitimate interpretations of the world. Although this relativisation might be regarded by religious relativists as advantageous for monotheism, it could have some unfavourable ramifications. For instance, the possibility and legitimacy of religious transmission – the activity of spreading monotheistic beliefs even among those who do not deem them true – may be challenged or contested. Furthermore, this type of alethic relativism appears to give rise to a legitimate plurality of relatively true religious and non-religious assumptions about the world.[3] Against this backdrop, it is not surprising that there has been a long-standing critique of relativism, or of certain versions of it, within monotheism, especially from the Catholic Church.

One could counter this line of reasoning by arguing that a relativist understanding of monotheism does not necessarily pose insurmountable problems for monotheists. Does it not, in contrast, offer manifold resources for addressing serious contemporary challenges to monotheism? For example, might truth relativism not provide an elegant solution to the problem of religious plurality, namely the fact that today there exist numerous and, at times, contradictory

---

[2] 'Absolutism' is the common antonym to 'relativism' in the philosophical debate. For the sake of simplicity, I use the terms 'absolute' and 'objective', concerning epistemological and ontological matters, interchangeably. A more precise analysis might point out that the former covers a broader semantic field and the distinction between the two is emphasised in moral philosophy and by some relativists.

[3] It is disputed between defenders and detractors of relativism whether the relativist is obliged to assert the 'equal validity' of the relativised perspectives or frameworks (Boghossian 2006: 2; Kusch 2020b: 4). We return to this point in Section 2.2.4.

religious truth claims in competition with one another? By assuming that not all of these claims can be objectively true at the same time, but that they may be relatively true (that is, for believers), interreligious disagreements and conflicts of faith seem to become easily resolvable. There are more arguments in favour of monotheistic relativism. Consider religious fundamentalism, intolerance, and violence. Does historical experience not amply demonstrate that these stances often arise from an exclusive insistence on a single God and one objective truth? Furthermore, if the monotheistic imperative of expansion is taken seriously, should this truth not ideally be recognised and believed by *all* people?

Through this line of thought, one can identify a few recent philosophical and theological concepts within the monotheistic traditions that either explicitly advocate a form of relativism or can be reasonably interpreted as relativistic. To the best of my knowledge, these concepts have emerged only within the framework of Christian monotheism. What are the motives for defending what Joseph Runzo, an American analytic philosopher of religion, calls 'Christian relativism'? Section 3 aims to answer this question by examining two approaches to monotheistic relativism, starting with Runzo. In his view, relativism provides the most robust philosophical theory for dealing with the contradictory truth claims of world religions. Another religious relativist perspective is championed by pragmatist philosopher and theologian James K. A. Smith. His view amounts to the thesis that truth relativism is 'heretical'. Smith argues that certain biblical teachings can only be elucidated through a relativist construal of the Christian faith. It should be noted in passing that our focus on specific approaches to monotheistic relativism does not preclude the possibility that some monotheists, either consciously or unconsciously, may hold relativistic notions of their own belief. Since there are no reliable empirical studies on this topic, we must leave this point open and focus on explicit accounts of monotheistic relativism.

Against this background, the decisive question arises as to which interpretation of the relationship between monotheism and relativism is convincing and appropriate. We cannot provide an answer without a more precise understanding of monotheism. Section 4 delves deeper into the monotheistic idea of a supreme and transcendent God, particularly within the framework of the Abrahamic religions – Judaism, Christianity, and Islam. Specifically, we examine this idea in terms of its historical emergence among the people of Israel and its theological implications for the concepts of divine revelation and monotheistic truth claims. Proceeding from there, we will attend to anti-relativist approaches to monotheism, especially those within the Catholic tradition.

Section 5 draws conclusions from our previous analysis concerning the central question of whether, and to what extent, relativist positions are compatible with the traditional conception of monotheism. Should we embrace relativism as a persuasive philosophical theory for the contemporary proclamation of monotheistic faith and for fostering interreligious reconciliation, as some religious relativists suggest? In contrast, should we deem the relativist doctrine detrimental or even pernicious to monotheism? Alternatively, are both stances, in a strict sense, inappropriate or erroneous, because the question of whether monotheism and relativism are compatible may be overly general and require further differentiation? This is broadly the nuanced position I intend to defend in this Cambridge Element.

First, I argue that normative relativism concerning metaphysical and moral matters is not compatible with traditional monotheism, as it undermines monotheistic principles such as theological absolutism and truth-objectivism. The substantiation of this argument is the main focus of this Element. Second, despite this incompatibility, there are other types and approaches to relativism that might relate differently to monotheism, and could even be compatible with it. Two versions will be briefly examined: truth relativism about subjective matters, such as taste or predilection, which is currently much debated; and descriptive relativism, a weak and empirical form of relativist thinking. Overall, the general thesis that monotheism is inherently incompatible with relativism seems inadequate and simplistic.

Finally, my investigation is not about criticising relativism and lauding monotheism, or vice versa, but only about clarifying their relationship.

2 What Is Relativism?

Relativism has become a particular subject of controversy in philosophy and the humanities over the past thirty years. While relativist ideas have been espoused recurrently throughout the history of philosophy from ancient Greece to modern times, there has been increasing scholarly interest in analysing and discussing relativist concepts and arguments in recent years. This section introduces the philosophical concept of relativism, providing an overview of its basic features, distinctions, and versions as well as some current debates on relativist ideas and approaches.

2.1 Resurgence of Relativism

Even though relativist ideas have been advocated since the Greek philosopher Protagoras in the fifth century BC, the term 'relativism' itself emerged in more recent times.[4] It is believed that the word 'relativism' originated in the nineteenth century. Its first known usage can be found in the work of the German philosopher Wilhelm Traugott Krug. In his 1838 *Handwörterbuch der philosophischen Wissenschaften*, Krug describes relativism as 'the assumption that everything which we experience and think (the self, the idea of reason, truth, morality, religion etc.) is only something relative, and therefore has no essential endurance and no universal validity' (Baghramian & Coliva 2020: 39).

Since ancient times, the agenda of relativism has been highly controversial. Certain critics perceive relativism, or certain versions thereof, as being 'true to nobody', as Plato suggested in his *Theaetetus* (Plato 1988: 111), or, more recently, as the 'main philosophical malady of our time' (Popper 2020: 485). In contrast, proponents view relativism as the only philosophical stance allowing 'faultless disagreement' (Kölbel 2002: 92), or they simply equate it with 'serious thought' (Fish 2001). In the United States during the 1990s, a line of dispute between critics and proponents of relativism had taken on the character of a 'culture war' with, at times, mutual defamation. A trigger for these disputes was the bestseller *The Closing of the American Mind* by the American philosopher and cultural critic Allan Bloom. This book extensively criticised the relativism and liberalism of North American university culture and society (Bloom 1987). Sociologist of religion Peter L. Berger makes the following diagnosis: 'Contemporary culture (and by no means only in America) appears to be in the grip of two seemingly contradictory forces. One pushes the culture towards relativism, the view that there are no absolutes whatever, that moral or philosophical truth is inaccessible if not illusory. The other pushes towards a militant and uncompromising affirmation of this or that (alleged) absolute truth' (Berger 2010: 1). Fortunately, the debate on relativism has evolved in recent years, leading to the emergence of more nuanced and less pugnacious and polarised positions.

Relativist ideas and theories are primarily discussed in four domains today. First, within analytic philosophy, there has been a broad debate on relativism for approximately twenty years, ranging from subtle and highly specialised versions of truth and semantic relativism to new approaches to metaphysical and moral relativism. In recent years, a multitude of anthologies, monographs, and articles on relativism have been published within the analytic discourse (Hales 2011; Baghramian 2014; Baghramian & Coliva 2020; Kusch 2020a). Second, ongoing debates on relativism exist in the fields of anthropology and social sciences, in which accounts of cultural relativism have been embraced as

---

[4] For the history of relativism, see Baghramian & Coliva (2020: 25–61), Irlenborn (2016: 19–40), and Kusch (2020a: 39–143).

a rejection of ethnocentrism and colonialism (Brown 2008; Park 2011). Third, debates on relativism have been conducted in political theory, particularly on the contentious topic of the universality of human rights. Recent contributions to this debate examine whether the traditionally asserted universality and egalitarian status of human rights can be justified against relativist objections (Corradetti 2022). Fourth, disputes about the challenges posed by relativist views have also been ignited with regard to monotheistic theology (Irlenborn & Seewald 2020). In the Catholic tradition, there has been a long-standing critique of relativist ideas, tracing back to documents of the Church's magisterium in the nineteenth century and culminating in recent times with the notorious phrase by former Cardinal Joseph Ratzinger (later Pope Benedict XVI) about a 'dictatorship of relativism' (Ratzinger 2005). Proponents of this stance face various theological and political positions that criticise Catholic anti-relativism as indicative of conservative anti-modernism or a general backwardness of Church positions (Perl 2007; Accetti 2015). As previously indicated, there are also theological and philosophical approaches, stemming from or influenced by Christian tradition, that assert the compatibility of relativism with Christian monotheism in certain respects.

The idea of relativism arose from philosophical deliberation and, as such, constitutes a genuine subject of philosophy. Philosophical relativism can be viewed as both a generalisation and a specification of common intuitions about relativity at an abstract level. Consider the following statements.

(a) This is true for you, but not for me.
(b) Each culture has its own moral standard.
(c) You cannot argue about taste.

Each statement, to varying degrees, expresses a specific relationship of dependence. Something is claimed to be relational to something else upon which it depends: (a) truth claims are related to individual judgements, (b) moral standards depend on cultural norms, and (c) taste relies on individual preferences. According to these statements, truth claims and moral standards are not true *simpliciter*; rather they are true relatively, in that they depend on specific contexts. Without further qualification, it is difficult to determine the extent to which these statements genuinely express relativist attitudes. Empirical research in the United States has reported a relativistic bias among adolescents (Smith 2011: 215–224). Many of those interviewed said it was inappropriate and intrusive to judge others and their behaviours; they believed no one had the right to impose their truth claims or moral standards on others. In contrast to such commonplace relativistic attitudes, relativism as a philosophical doctrine operates at a much more abstract and theoretical level. Nevertheless, the notion of dependency remains at the core of philosophical relativism, albeit in a more specific way than in everyday notions of relativity.

The intrinsic connection between the ideas of relativism and dependency is also hinted at in the etymology of the term 'relativism'. It stems from the Latin past participle passive *relatus*, which derives from the verb *refero*, meaning 'to carry back'. This etymological background of 'relativism' suggests that to evaluate the truth of a belief X, one must 'carry it back' to Y, the domain from which it originates and upon which it depends. Consequently, the truth claim of X is explained solely within the context of Y, and only within this context can X be considered and accepted as true. To this extent, the imperative of 'carrying back' challenges the idea of a universal or objective truth, instead affirming its relative and dependent nature.

Even though the term 'relativism' is broadly used in contemporary philosophy, it remains highly ambiguous. Relativists repeatedly refer to three key concepts to underscore its significance: 'pluralism', 'tolerance', and 'scepticism'. In brief, pluralism suggests that in our globalised world, claims to objective truth are increasingly untenable, necessitating a relativisation of truth claims. Tolerance can be described as an attitude towards accepting foreign beliefs or practices even when they diverge from one's own. Advocates of relativism argue in various ways that respecting these diverse perspectives requires a relativisation of one's own standpoint. They frequently criticise fundamentalism, which imposes its purported absolute truth claims on others in an intolerant and often coercive or violent manner. Scepticism, another pillar of relativism, challenges the idea of an absolute or objective truth as potentially excessive, contradictory, or illusory, given the fallibility of all human knowledge.

Opponents of relativism typically advance two arguments. First, relativism should be regarded as an inconsistent and inherently self-refuting doctrine. A relativist commits a self-contradiction by denying objective truth while, simultaneously, presupposing it in the assertion that all truth is relative. The relativist thesis is either relative or non-relative. If deemed relative, it becomes merely one thesis among many, requiring no further attention beyond its limited scope. If deemed non-relative, the relativist paradoxically asserts something that is simultaneously denied: an objective, non-relative truth. In simplified terms, this is the well-known accusation of 'self-refutation' against relativism, which has been repeatedly articulated from Plato to the present day. Relativist philosophers have attempted to refute it with intricate semantic and logical arguments (Kölbel 2011; Hales 2020). Many scholars involved in the debate argue that the so-called 'standard' objection does not necessarily result in the self-refutation of global relativism for various reasons. For these scholars, it is difficult to explain why relativistic positions continue to exist, even though this argument has been invoked in various forms since Plato. This is interpreted as an indication that the self-refutation argument is not capable of refuting relativism. The following statement by Alasdair MacIntyre is frequently quoted in this context: 'For relativism, like scepticism, is one of those doctrines that have by now been refuted a number of times too often. [...] Genuinely refutable doctrines only need to be refuted once' (MacIntyre 1985: 5). Of course, this historically motivated critique of the self-refutation argument can also be reversed: If it has been repeatedly raised against versions of global relativism since antiquity, it does not seem to be entirely without merit. However, the 'standard' objection may bolster an anti-relativist position by uncovering weaknesses in a specific relativist approach and demonstrating that it remains a less compelling theory.

Second, relativism could have detrimental consequences for the notion of progress in knowledge. Philosophical and scientific pursuits typically focus not on whether epistemological claims are true relative to a specific framework or parameter but on whether they are objectively true, regardless of whether someone holds them to be true. If the quest for truth was solely concerned with the analysis of relativised parameters, philosophy would focus exclusively on clarifying questions of dependence rather than addressing questions of fact. In science, this approach could lead to the notion that knowledge is dependent on specific contexts of interpretation, which would undermine both the concept of objective scientific truth and the expectation of verifiable progress in knowledge. Given these divergent perspectives, it is not surprising that proponents and opponents of relativism often cannot even agree on the basic idea of what this term should mean in the first place, let alone its precise definition. Some relativists have expressed concerns that absolutists are inclined to formulate a biased definition of relativism from the outset, aiming to demonstrate that relativist positions are contradictory or unpersuasive. In this respect, David Bloor, a prominent relativist in the sociology of scientific knowledge, warns that, often, '[a]nti-relativists treat relativists as foolish persons who believe foolish things or who are committed to foolish things without realising it' (Bloor 2011: 452). The difficulty in finding an acceptable definition for both relativists and absolutists is partly due to the semantic ambiguity of the term 'relativism', which covers a multitude of ideas and issues across all areas of philosophy. Hence, attempting to define a single concept or theory of relativism that applies to all its types and versions appears unrealistic and overly ambitious. Participants in the debate often identify only some core features of relativism that are deemed essential, either for the general concept or for a particular version, such as epistemic or moral relativism. Overall, even the attempt to outline a concept of relativism is likely to spark further discussion.

2.2 On the Concept of Relativism

Relativist approaches revolve around the idea 'X is relative to Y'. Of course, not everyone who claims that X is relative to Y is a relativist. Understood in a relativistic sense and with reference to truth, it roughly means that X (a belief, proposition, statement, assertion, norm, value, etc.) is not true objectively but only relatively, depending on a particular parameter Y (a worldview, cognitive scheme, conceptual framework, culture, language, belief system, etc.). More specifically, in terms of the assertion 'X is relative to Y', a basic model of normative relativism can be formulated as follows (for simplicity, I will use 'belief'[5] for 'X' in the subsequent discussion):

(1) Beliefs, either in a given domain or globally, are not true or false objectively but only relatively, depending on particular frameworks.
(2) A belief can be, at the same time and in the same sense, true relative to framework Y and false relative to a different framework Z.
(3) There are no non-relative or absolute standards for judging whether frameworks Y, Z, or others are objectively true or false.
(4) Consequently, all beliefs within their respective domains hold equal validity, as they are all true in a relative sense.

This general model serves as the basis for our analysis of relativism. Without further conceptual clarifications and recourse to specific relativist approaches, however, it is only to a certain extent meaningful to speak thus broadly about relativism.

In terms of conceptual clarification, the model allows us to identify and examine some core features of normative relativism that are interconnected and partially overlap in meaning. In short, thesis (1) states that relativist beliefs express a relation of *dependency*, as they are not true independently but only in reference to, or depending upon, specific contexts, frameworks, perspectives, etc. Thesis (2) reflects the relativist's strategy of *conflict resolution* by relating beliefs to particular frameworks, thereby settling disagreements between

---

[5] The term 'belief' is understood here as an assertion that something is true or false, not as a psychological or performative attitude or disposition. For instance, the belief that 'There is a supreme God' can be considered true or false, depending on whether what it asserts really obtains. A proposition is commonly defined as something that is asserted or expressed by a belief. Thus, the belief 'There is a supreme God' expresses the proposition or the propositional content that a supreme God exists. To this extent, beliefs can be termed 'true' or 'false' due to their propositional contents (Alston 1996: 1–2).

conflicting or incompatible positions based on (1). Thesis (3) refers to *non-absolutism*, since relativism – based on (1) and (2) – denies the existence of a neutral and absolute standpoint, as well as non-relative standards for adjudicating a belief or framework as objectively true. Thesis (4) draws the epistemological consequences from (1) to (3), suggesting that although a normative relativist may be inclined to somehow favour his or her position over competing proposals, there seem to be no conceptual resources available to contest the *equal validity* of these competing relativist and non-relativist approaches.

In recent debates, both critics and defenders of relativism have presented various lists of what they deem core features of 'relativism' (Baghramian & Coliva 2020: 6–11) or of a specific version of it, such as 'epistemic relativism' (Kusch 2020b: 2–4). It should be noted that by formulating certain features of relativism, one directly engages with controversial terrain. The number of features involved and their scope of application vary, depending on the stance. Some relativists and absolutists might reject certain features and prefer others; therefore, it is difficult to find common ground. While Baghramian and Coliva, for example, assert that their list of six features ('non-absolutism', 'dependence', 'multiplicity', 'incompatibility', 'equal validity', and 'non-neutrality') applies to 'all accounts of relativism' (Baghramian & Coliva 2020: 6), Kusch identifies five features that must be agreed upon for a position to qualify as relativism: 'dependence', 'non-absolutism', 'plurality', 'conflict', and 'non-neutrality' (Kusch 2019: 273).

Our analysis of relativism will focus on the four features mentioned previously, as they are, in my view, the most relevant for exploring the correlation between relativism and monotheism. While two of these features, 'dependency' and 'non-absolutism', are also recognised in the lists of both Kusch and Baghramian & Coliva, 'equal validity' remains controversial, as some relativists reject it. The 'conflict resolution' feature is my own addition. I contend that these four features are necessary conditions for common versions of normative relativism, without claiming that they are both necessary and sufficient conditions, or that they apply as necessary conditions for all existing or conceivable types of normative relativism. In the following discussion, I will briefly explain these four features, focussing particularly on the controversial feature 'equal validity'

2.2.1 Dependency

As previously outlined, relativism is centred on a specific dependency relationship among beliefs that relativists claim to have discovered. The thesis 'X is relative to Y' formally implies an asymmetrical relationship between the two variables or relata, X and Y, with the former being dependent on the latter but not vice versa. This relationship of dependence can be analysed in three respects: first, concerning the dependent relatum X; second, concerning the independent relatum Y; and third, concerning the relation between the two (Irlenborn 2016: 9–12).

Concerning the first and second points, in the debate on relativism scholars have frequently presented schemes or classifications containing examples of the relata X and Y (O'Grady 2002: 4; Baghramian 2004: 8; Baghramian & Carter 2020; Kusch 2020b: 1–2). Philosopher Susan Haack's proposed scheme is frequently cited (Haack 1998: 149). This scheme can be seen as:

IS RELATIVE TO
(1) meaning	(a) language
(2) reference	(b) conceptual scheme
(3) truth	(c) theory
(4) metaphysical commitment	(d) scientific paradigm
(5) ontology	(e) version, depiction, description
(6) reality	(f) culture
(7) epistemic values	(g) community
(8) moral values	(h) individual
(9) aesthetic values	

Combinations of elements from both sets of relata in 'X is relative to Y' offer various possible relativist positions. For instance, combining (3) with (c) might lead to a version of truth relativism, (1) with (f) to a version of cultural relativism, and (8) with (g) to moral relativism, among others. Not all combinations yield meaningful versions of relativism. As Haack rightly notes, claiming that moral values (8) are relative to scientific paradigms (d) would not make sense. Nevertheless, combinations of these relata have been advocated by notable philosophers. For instance, Benjamin Whorf's linguistic relativism can be described as a combination of relata (1), (5), and (6) with (a). Richard Rorty's epistemic relativism can be interpreted as a conjunction of (7) with (f) and (g), whereas Paul Feyerabend's scientific relativism combines (1) with (c) and (d). Additionally, regarding relata (a) to (h), it is possible to distinguish between abstract nouns such as language, theory, culture, paradigm, and conceptual scheme, and concrete nouns, which, like (g) and (h), denote an individual or community, respectively.

Concerning the third point, the philosophical discussion of dependency relations, which partly touches on complex metaphysical matters (Tahko & Lowe 2020), reveals various ways in which one object may depend on another. Within this discourse, two fundamental distinctions relevant to our topic have led to different types of relativism.

1. The first distinction is between *descriptive* and *normative* relativism. Descriptive relativism typically posits empirical claims about the relativity of beliefs among individuals or groups across different languages, modes of thought, cultures, societies, or religions. For descriptive relativists, beliefs within a specific domain are significantly shaped, influenced, and determined by these varying contexts. Accordingly, in terms of 'X is relative to Y', the descriptive relativist asserts to have identified an empirical parameter Y – either a historical, cultural, or religious context – upon which X is thought to depend. It is important to note that this weak form of relativism merely aims at *describing* the dependency of X on Y as an empirical observation of how the world is in this respect, without making any evaluative judgements. Given this, in light of our topic, an example of descriptive relativism is the assertion that 'The concept of a single transcendent God is relative to specific monotheistic religions'.

By contrast, normative relativism prescribes a non-empirical norm according to which a belief X is dependent on a framework Y. In this context, the dependency is considered normative, meaning that it should apply universally and without exception. More precisely, normative relativism stipulates a principle whereby X is not regarded as true in an objective sense, but as invariably relative to, and dependent upon, framework Y. Consider the example: 'Religious doctrines are always only true relative to a particular belief system'. This assertion does not stem from an empirical investigation of how all extant and conceivable religious doctrines can be described; rather, it comes from the norm of how these doctrines ought to be conceived. Strikingly, while most normative relativists are likely to be descriptive relativists, the reverse is not necessarily true. Theoretically, descriptive relativists might endorse normative absolutism in the same domain. For instance, even if the concept of a single God is empirically relative to particular monotheistic religions, a descriptive relativist might nevertheless consider one of these religions to be absolutely true.

One could argue that descriptive relativism possesses limited philosophical relevance. It seems to express less a genuine form of relativism and more a type of pluralism or relationalism, which refers to the multifaceted or relational nature of reality. However, this objection may not be sufficiently persuasive. Subsequently, I am inclined to regard descriptive relativism as a genuine and meaningful form of relativism, particularly in light of the analysis of religious diversity. At least three arguments can be advanced in support of descriptive relativism. First, some philosophers, such as Immanuel Kant, contend that, in contrast to descriptive relativism, a priori knowledge is accessible to all human beings. This perspective makes the factual differences in cognitive standpoints across a plurality of cultures or religions hardly conceivable or understandable (Swoyer 2010: chap. 1.2). Second, descriptive relativism may facilitate the recognition of empirical contingency in the adoption of beliefs. Third, descriptive relativism may foster epistemic modesty when engaging with diverse worldviews. We revisit the latter two points in Section 5.

2. The second distinction is between *global* and *local* relativism. The former relates the dependency of X on Y (in 'X is relative to Y') to *all* classes of beliefs or propositions, while the latter restricts it to a class of beliefs or propositions within a specific domain, such as ontology, morality, religion, science, or aesthetics. Global dependency implies global relativism, while local dependency entails local relativism. Global relativism, rarely represented in the debate, maintains that X is relative to Y across all possible domains, whereas local relativism asserts that the dependency of X on Y is confined to a specific domain. The assertion 'Truth is always relative' exemplifies global relativism, while 'Scientific knowledge is relative to a particular paradigm' represents an instance of local relativism, specifically within the philosophy of science. It should be noted that local relativism in one domain may be compatible with local absolutism in another. For instance, one could be a local relativist in the domain of aesthetics and, at the same time, maintain a local absolutist position in the domain of metaphysics. Of course, not all combinations of local relativism and absolutism are plausible. For example, it is unlikely that someone would simultaneously hold moral absolutism and epistemic relativism.

2.2.2 Conflict Resolution

In accordance with truth relativism, beliefs in a specific domain are invariably true only in a relative sense. Consequently, a belief can be, at the same time and in the same sense, true *and* false, relative to different parameters. Indeed, there may be domains in which beliefs possess truth values only relative to certain frameworks or assessment parameters, namely concerning matters of taste and aesthetic preferences. For instance, the assertion 'Pinot blanc wine is delicious' might be simultaneously true for Tom and false for Lynn. Although Tom and Lynn disagree, both positions would be considered true, thus appearing equally valid. This implies that the same belief could have different truth values depending on the assessment of the individuals for whom it is either relatively true or false.

Over the past two decades, a broad and widely recognised debate has emerged concerning this type of alethic relativism in matters of subjective taste and preference. It was prompted by a group of relativists, whose concept has since been mostly referred to as 'New Relativism' (Baghramian & Carter 2020: chap. 5). Notably, these 'new' relativists do not focus on 'disputes of fact' in terms of empirical or metaphysical matters. Instead, they focus on 'disputes of inclination' (Wright 2010: 340), which revolve around semantic difficulties arising from disagreement on matters of subjective taste. In this context, 'new' relativists conceive of relativism as a set of 'views which allow two judgements to disagree while both being correct, in some objective sense' (MacFarlane 2022: 500). This notion has since been termed 'faultless disagreement' by some 'new' relativists (Kölbel 2002: 92). Based on a concept of relative truth (García-Carpintero & Kölbel 2008), some 'new' relativists assert that they take genuine disagreement seriously and aim to resolve conflicts of belief in such a way that neither disputing party commits an epistemic error. Accordingly, judgements in 'disputes of inclination' are not true *simpliciter* or objectively, but only in a relative sense. Thus, 'Pinot blanc wine is delicious' is true for Tom relative to his standard of truth (or 'context of assessment'), but it is false for Lynn relative to her standard. In Section 5, we explore whether this version of truth relativism has any bearing on monotheistic belief.

Steven D. Hales, an advocate of truth relativism, has stated that 'relativism is a way to resolve disagreement' (Hales 2014: 63). For him, '[r]elativism as a solution to disagreement is adequately motivated when (1) we have uncovered a genuine irreconcilable difference, a disagreement that is epistemically irresolvable because there is no such thing as the right kind of evidence to settle it, and (2) the alternative solutions to disagreement are not available' (Hales 2014: 77). Hales argues that relativism offers the only successful conflict-resolving strategy, even in matters of truth and justification (Hales 2014: 82). How can we comprehend these two assertions? With reference to our topic, consider the belief T: 'There is a supreme God'. According to our basic model, the relativist's default position would be that T is true relative to the belief system of a monotheist M and false relative to the belief system of a polytheist P. As T would be true for M and false for P, a disagreement between M and P might arise, given that both belief systems are incompatible. There are at least two ways in which the relativist on religious truth claims could resolve the disagreement between M and P.

First, the relativist might adopt contextualism. Roughly, contextualism encompasses views holding that utterances and expressions about knowledge and truth can only be understood relative to specified contexts. Accordingly, the utterance 'that T' would not express one singular belief or proposition, but *two*, each relative to a different parameter or belief system: 'There is a supreme God relative to the belief system of M', and 'There is no supreme God relative to the belief system of P'. By relativising the content of the utterance to different contexts, the contextual relativist could claim that the two beliefs or propositions are co-tenable. They neither contradict each other nor violate the principle of non-contradiction, which states that contradictory beliefs or propositions cannot be true at the same time and in the same sense. Furthermore, this construal does not lead to a disagreement or conflict between M and P. What should we make of this approach? In brief, even if the contextualist might successfully demonstrate the faultlessness of both positions, she fails because her proposal simply explains away what is at stake here for both non-contextual relativists and absolutists: the genuine disagreement and belief conflict between M and P. Contextualism seems unable to capture and represent the familiar notion that a disagreement appears genuine only when there is a 'common subject matter and consequently *shared content* between the parties of the disagreement' (Lynch 2011: 89). This is the basis for the critique that '[c]ontextualism is relativism tamed' (Williamson 2005: 91).

Second, the relativist could interpret the utterance 'that T' as representing a single belief or proposition, affirmed by M and rejected by P. Consequently, the same belief would be, simultaneously and in the same sense, true relative to the belief system of M and false relative to that of P. This approach would acknowledge what Hales described as an 'irreconcilable difference'. However, in light of the law of non-contradiction, one might question whether a relativist's position is ultimately convincing. Would it truly be plausible for M and P to accept this conflict as 'epistemically irresolvable'? Moreover, regarding Hales's second requirement, are there truly no 'alternative solutions' to this interreligious disagreement other than normative relativism? Section 5 addresses these questions.

2.2.3 Non-Absolutism

Regarding normative truth relativism, not only is every belief considered relatively true or false, depending on a specific parameter, but each parameter is also deemed relatively true or false, depending upon a higher-order parameter. In our model of relativism, thesis (2) states that a belief can be, at the same time and in the same sense, true relative to framework Y and false relative to framework Z. For the relativist, Y and Z are likewise not objectively true, but only relative to further parameters. With regard to the latter aspect, the American philosopher Paul Boghossian has claimed that references to further parameters might lead the relativist into a 'looming regress' of ever-new parameters at each stage, which would ultimately make the relativist construal of our utterances incomprehensible (Boghossian 2006: 56).

As we have seen, for normative truth relativism, no non-relative or absolute standards are available to objectively or independently justify a belief or parameter as true. This constraint highlights why the antonym of relativism is 'absolutism', a view that maintains the existence of absolute facts, truths, or values in respective domains. In line with the etymology of 'relativism' mentioned earlier, absolutism implies that for a belief to be comprehended, it does not need to be 'carried back' to its originating context, upon which its truth or validity purportedly depends, but is instead 'detached' from it (the meaning of the Latin term *absolutus*). Absolutism can occur in various forms. In terms of semantics, absolutism typically asserts that a belief or proposition is true if it applies independently of our holding it to be true – that is, at all times, in all places, and for all subjects, regardless of whether they acknowledge it. In this sense, 'true absolutely' means irrelative to specific parameters or perspectives, and even if no one is aware of this truth. In terms of epistemology, absolutism generally holds that there are epistemic standards which justify beliefs or render them true independent of our conceptions. In terms of ethics, absolutists presume the existence of moral principles that are objectively or universally true or false, without depending on specific moral codes or parameters (for simplicity, distinctions such as between moral absolutism and moral objectivism are not addressed here). In terms of metaphysics, absolutists might argue that there are mind-independent or absolute facts that render a belief or proposition true. A fact is considered absolute or objective when 'it obtains independently of whether anyone knows, believes, or is aware that it obtains' (Sankey 2022: 118). However, speaking of objective facts does not imply that absolutists rely on a bizarre 'God's eye view' – a perspective with knowledge only an omniscient being could possess – but rather acknowledges a form of perspectivism. This qualification implies that 'we must perceive absolute facts from a perspective, but this does not enter into facts' (Sankey 2022: 117). As noted in the introduction, traditional monotheism defends a version of theological absolutism concerning its central truth claim: the existence of a supreme and transcendent God as an absolute fact.

In this regard, the alethic relativist denies what the absolutist defends: the existence of absolute facts in a given domain that serve as truth-makers for claims about being. As Bloor succinctly puts it, 'To be relativist is to deny that there is such a thing as absolute knowledge and absolute truth' (Bloor 2011: 436). According to him, 'non-absolutism' suffices as a necessary and sufficient condition for normative relativism (Bloor 2020: 389). Overall, 'non-absolutism' is perhaps the least controversial feature of the debate between the defenders and critics of relativism.

2.2.4 Equal Validity

Given that beliefs and parameters within a specific domain are inherently true (or false) only in a relative sense – without any neutral and objective standards to determine which of two conflicting positions is non-relatively true (or false) – all beliefs, according to normative relativism, must be regarded as equally valid, since they uniformly possess only a relative status of truth. While the first three features of relativism we have discussed are recognised by most relativists (Kusch 2020b: 2–4), 'equal validity' remains highly controversial. Paul

Boghossian, a critic of epistemic relativism, has introduced this concept. For him, epistemic relativism is bound to accept what he calls 'the doctrine of equal validity' (Boghossian 2006: 3): 'There are many radically different, yet "equally valid" ways of knowing the world, with science being just one of them.' Boghossian posits that the 'equal validity' view has considerable influence in the humanities and social sciences. When applied to factual matters, such as the former existence of dinosaurs or the number of moons the planet Mars has, Boghossian deems this doctrine 'radical' and 'counterintuitive' (Boghossian 2006: 5). Other critics extended the scope of this critique beyond its epistemic relativism. For them, each form of normative relativism 'is committed to holding that different and incompatible viewpoints in any area of discourse for which this doctrine [of equal validity] has been invoked are legitimate *at least in principle*' (Baghramian & Coliva 2020: 24).

On the one hand, several relativist approaches have revolved around the idea of incommensurability, which may be compatible with the thesis of equal validity; some may even support it without explicitly stating so. The notorious term 'incommensurability', introduced by philosophers of science Thomas S. Kuhn and Paul Feyerabend, sparked various debates on cultural and scientific relativism during the 1970s and 1980s. According to Kuhn and Feyerabend, two theories are considered incommensurable if they are so deeply entrenched in opposing conceptual frameworks that there are no common standards to compare them (and, we might add, to deny the equal validity of the other theory) or to translate the terms of one theory into those of another.

A few years ago, the American philosopher Carol Rovane took up this notion of incommensurability, presenting a widely discussed account of many-world relativism, which she calls 'multimundialism' (Rovane 2013: 10). Significantly, Rovane criticises what she terms the '*Disagreement Intuition*' or '*Relative Truth Intuition*' of 'New Relativism' (Rovane 2013: 5), according to which relativism, as outlined previously, occurs with supposedly irresoluble disagreement. She contrasts this 'intuition' with her '*Alternatives Intuition*' (Rovane 2013: 6), which suggests the existence of a multitude of insulated worlds. In essence, Rovane posits a plurality of truths that cannot be embraced together, as they are relative to alternative and incommensurable metaphysical worlds. According to her argument, the inhabitants of one of these worlds must perceive with 'profound *epistemic indifference*' (Rovane 2013: 10) what lies outside of their own realm.

> We shall have to acknowledge that the truth-value bearers that are outside of the boundaries within which we operate are not candidates for belief by us; and we shall have to acknowledge as well that we have nothing to teach, and

nothing to learn from, other people who reside outside of those boundaries – that is the practical implication of their inhabiting a different world. (Rovane 2013: 10)

However, this relativistic scenario may not appear particularly promising. Although Rovane has not explicitly addressed the feature of 'equal validity', it can be inferred as a necessary component of her 'multimundialism'. Given the 'profound *epistemic indifference*' among these enclosed and insulated worlds, the inhabitants of world A would lack the resources to claim that truth exists only in A, and that other worlds like B and C are not 'equally valid' in terms of truth. Since there is no neutral ground upon which to adjudicate between the incompatible truth claims of worlds A, B, C, and so forth, these alternative and incommensurable worlds must be regarded as 'equally valid' from a relativist perspective.

On the other hand, many relativists explicitly reject 'equal validity' as a necessary feature of relativism. For instance, the epistemic relativist Martin Kusch points out that '[m]ost card-carrying relativists' would deny it (Kusch 2020b: 4). Similarly, David Bloor insists that the relativist is not committed, as Boghossian suggested, to saying to the absolutist that the relativist standards 'are no more correct than yours'. Instead, he may assert: 'I acknowledge that my standards are no more *absolute* than yours' (Bloor 2020: 391).

It would be too extensive to elaborate further on the arguments for and against the 'equal validity' thesis here. In my view, it seems inconsistent for relativists to deny this as a feature of relativism. Bloor's remark that the relativist assures the absolutist 'that my standards are no more *absolute* than yours' seems more like an escape from the problem than an answer to it. Considering all four features of relativism, a relativist who rejects 'equal validity' might be faced with the following problem. By criticising absolutism and defending relativism, she inevitably prefers her own relativist stance to other, non-relativist, approaches. However, how is this preference justifiable, given that, according to normative truth relativism, all approaches in a certain domain are true only in a relative sense? The relativist thus seems compelled to adopt the view that her position is 'relatively more true' than that of the absolutist. In other words, as a prerequisite for prioritising their own approach over others, relativists appear to implicitly rely on degrees of truth concerning the spectrum of relative true positions.

If this reasoning is correct, it would be reasonable for the relativist to accept the thesis of 'equal validity'. Otherwise, the relativist would face the unpleasant task of clarifying what the intermediate truth value 'relatively more true' (and 'relatively less true') is supposed to mean. Notably, the notion of gradual truth values is highly controversial in semantics and logic. At this point, the relativist seems to be confronted with a dilemma: either relativism is, in Bloor's words, 'no more correct' than absolutism, or it is not. Regarding the latter idea, the relativist must demonstrate that his approach is somehow superior to that of the non-relativist. Given that all approaches are only relatively true, the relativist must resort to something akin to gradual truth values to justify this claim. As suggested, this strategy is unlikely to be promising or persuasive. Regarding the former idea, the relativist would affirm 'equal validity' as a necessary feature of his approach. Since this option appears most convincing and coherent for the relativist, I shall continue to regard 'equal validity' as a necessary feature of normative relativism.

2.3 Versions and Approaches

The analysis of the basic model has provided a preliminary overview of the agenda of normative relativism and some related current debates. The hitherto general analysis allowed us to incorporate various, sometimes incompatible, relativist positions, such as approaches based on irresolvable disagreement, as opposed to approaches relying on the concept of 'multimundialism'. Moving forward, we will focus more specifically on selected relativist versions that are relevant to the relationship between monotheism and relativism.

2.3.1 Alethic or Truth Relativism

Alethic relativism encompasses philosophical views that typically assert there are no objective or absolute truths. According to this position, the truth of beliefs is always relative to and dependent upon specific frameworks. In other words, the truth of a belief is bound to a particular viewpoint, and there exists no non-relative stance from which to adjudicate objectively among competing truth claims. This notion of truth relativism forms the core idea underlying most relativist approaches and versions. Relativists have consistently asserted that truths within specific domains such as logic, epistemology, or morality should be considered relative. However, an exception to this correlation between truth and relativism is the relativistically inclined expressivism. This non-cognitive position argues that beliefs about moral, religious, or aesthetic matters do not relate to facts and lack truth values. Instead, they express the subjective attitudes or value judgements of the speaker (Beddor 2020).

The significance of the term 'truth' in alethic relativism, along with the criteria applied to it, and its association with specific theories of truth, have not been addressed in the previous discussions. In principle, alethic relativism is not committed to any particular theory of truth. However, most proponents of alethic relativism tend to favour an epistemic conception of truth, while rejecting the non-epistemic model. In brief, the two positions can be outlined as follows:

– *Non-epistemic* or *realist* theories of truth assume that the truth of a belief (a proposition or statement) is not necessarily dependent on our epistemic ability to ascertain, justify, or verify it. A belief is deemed true if, and only if, what it asserts is indeed the case.

– *Epistemic* or *anti-realist* theories of truth contend that the truth of a belief, under epistemically favourable conditions, is dependent on our epistemic ability to hold it as true, specifically through sufficient ascertainment, justification, or verification.

Non-epistemic theories do not claim that the truth of *all* beliefs is non-epistemic. Generally, they suggest – often in reference to ambiguous or hitherto unexplained facts about the spatiotemporal world – that there are beliefs whose truth values remain indeterminate, or they may not be precisely verifiable at present. Such beliefs *may* be true, even if we are epistemically unable to conclusively verify them.

These two conceptions of truth are based on different responses to the question of whether there is an objective reality that is causally independent of our epistemic access and can serve as the truth-maker for certain beliefs (Alston 1996: 5). In various versions, realism proceeds from the basic idea that objects within a specific area of reality are causally independent of the human mind (*ontological realism*). For realists, mental access (through cognition, knowledge, or true beliefs) to the properties of objects within this thought-independent reality is fundamentally possible, enabling us, in principle, to recognise them (approximately) as they truly are (*epistemological realism*) and articulate true assertions about them (*semantical realism*). In contrast, anti-realism challenges these assumptions in various ways. Some forms of anti-realism even deny the existence of a mind-independent reality. Other forms acknowledge the existence of mind-independent objects within certain domains, such as macroscopic objects and their properties, yet argue that we lack epistemic access to this world, precluding any form of correspondence between this mind-independent reality and our beliefs about it. For most anti-realists, the concept of a mind-independent world is meaningless, as they contend that the difference between a thought-independent and a thought-dependent world always solely depends on thought.

Although there are close connections between relativism and anti-realism, it is crucial to distinguish these positions for various reasons (Bilgrami 2010; Norris 2011). Not every relativist is an anti-realist, not every anti-realist is a relativist, and, similarly, not every absolutist is a realist. Furthermore, there is no categorical distinction between both positions, as one can adopt a more or less realist or anti-realist stance regarding a specific subject matter (Miller 2021). Nonetheless, it can be assumed that alethic relativism, to put it cautiously, tends towards an epistemic notion of truth, as both views argue for the relativisation of truth to specific frameworks and against the existence of objective facts in a mind-independent world as truth-makers for beliefs and propositions.

These concepts and distinctions are pivotal to our topic. To assess the impact of relativism on monotheism, it is essential to understand the relationship between monotheistic truth claims and their referents. For instance, to comprehend the basic ideas of monotheism, we must address the question of what, according to the monotheistic doctrine, serves as the truth-maker for its central claim that a supreme God exists. In terms of non-epistemic theories of truth, the metaphysical belief 'There is a supreme God' is true if, and only if, such a supreme God actually exists, even if we lack the epistemic means to conclusively justify or verify his existence. In other words, within realist theories of truth, the fact that such a supreme God exists renders this belief true. In terms of epistemic theories of truth, the belief that a supreme God exists is true if, and only if, we have the epistemic ability to ascertain, justify, or verify it. In summary, although some relativist and anti-realist currents within the monotheistic tradition reject mainstream theological realism and absolutism, traditional monotheism generally aligns with a non-epistemic or realist notion of truth (as further explored in Sections 4 and 5).

2.3.2 Logical, Epistemic, and Moral Relativism

As previously indicated, besides alethic relativism, various other relativist versions exist, such as logical, moral, epistemic, scientific, and aesthetic relativism. Formally, these versions emerge from combinations of elements from the two sets of relata, as outlined in Section 2.2.1. These relativist versions can be formulated as specifications and extensions of our general relativism model.

Dependency	Beliefs *about logical, moral, epistemic, scientific, or aesthetic matters* are not true or false objectively but only relatively, depending on specific frameworks.
Conflict Resolution	A belief can be, at the same time and in the same sense, true relative to framework Y and false relative to a different framework Z.
Non-Absolutism	There are no non-relative or absolute standards for judging whether frameworks Y, Z, or others are objectively true or false.
Equal Validity	Consequently, all beliefs *about logical, moral, epistemic, scientific, or aesthetic matters* hold equal validity within their respective domains, as they are all true in a relative sense.

Accordingly, a position asserting that claims in the domain of morality (on moral matters) are not true objectively but only relatively would be considered 'moral relativism', while a position maintaining that claims in the domain of epistemic matters are not true objectively but only relatively would be categorised as 'epistemic relativism'. Due to space limitations, I shall briefly focus on three major versions of relativism.

Logical relativism: Logical relativism can be regarded as either a distinct version of relativism or as a form of alethic relativism. Some logical relativists posit that systems of logic are not objectively true. The underlying idea is usually that various, often incompatible, logical systems exist that are only relatively true, depending on factors such as culture, community, and subject matter. In this sense, it is asserted that beliefs and propositions depend on the specific logical systems being used. Classical logic, therefore, would be regarded merely as one among various, mostly divergent and frequently incompatible, logical systems, such as paraconsistent logic, multi-valued logic, and even Jain or Buddhist logic. Consequently, a belief concerning a logical matter could, at the same time and in the same sense, be true relative to, for instance, Buddhist logic, and false relative to classical logic. The relativisation of classical logic seems to offer several advantages for logical relativists.

As is widely known, classical logic encompasses three fundamental laws or principles of thought. Briefly, the bivalence principle asserts that every belief or proposition necessarily holds only one of two truth values: it is either true or false. The principle of non-contradiction states that two contradictory beliefs cannot be true at the same time and in the same sense. Lastly, the principle of the excluded middle posits that there is no third value between the two truth values 'true' and 'false' (in Latin: *tertium non datur*); for any given belief, either this belief or its negation must be true. In contrast to these classical logic principles, multi-valued logical systems presume the existence of more than two truth values (Gottwald 2015). In addition to 'true' and 'false', values such as 'indeterminate', 'mostly true', 'incongruent', or '0.67 true' (if numerical degrees between truth as '1' and falsity as '0' are allowed) might be considered as third truth values. Consequently, a *tertium*, or a third option between 'true' and 'false' becomes possible, providing relativists with a way to circumvent contradictions.

The American philosopher and logical relativist Joseph Margolis, for example, argues that

> every relativism [...] features two essential doctrines: (1) that, in formal terms, truth-values logically weaker than bipolar value (true and false) may be admitted to govern otherwise coherent forms of inquiry and constative acts, and (2) that substantively, not merely for evidentiary or epistemic reasons, certain sectors of the real world open to constative inquiry may be shown to support only such weaker truth-values. (Margolis 2010: 100)

According to Margolis, one should not universalise a single logical system such as classical logic. In his view, it is necessary to use the specific logical system that best suits the field or object under investigation. In terms of aesthetic disputes, for instance, Margolis considers a multi-valued logic to be far more suitable than a binary one. In such cases, he recommends abandoning classical logic's principles of thought (Margolis 2010: 104, 118; for a critique see O'Grady 2002: 33–35). With regard to our topic, Margolis's approach prompts the question of whether religion should also be considered a domain in which classical logic must be abandoned. If believers refrained from immediately labelling foreign belief systems incompatible with their own as 'false', and instead assessed them as, say, 'mostly true' or 'more true', this might foster religious tolerance and enhance spiritual progress among the diverse array of world religions. We will explore this further when we examine Joseph Runzo's approach in Section 3.

Epistemic relativism: Epistemic relativism roughly holds that claims about justification and knowledge are only true relatively, not objectively. Epistemic relativists generally argue that standards of knowledge and justification of beliefs invariably depend on specific epistemic frameworks or cognitive norms, which vary across historical, political, cultural, local, or religious contexts. Thus, they frequently presuppose different and often incompatible systems, sets, and standards of epistemic justification. Correspondingly, epistemic relativists dismiss the idea of non-relative or absolute standards for judging whether a particular cognitive framework or norm is objectively true (or false). According to epistemic relativism, there can be no 'God's eye view' that provides a supposedly objective truth over all relative and framework-dependent truth claims, given the finite human capacity for cognition. Epistemic relativism comes in various versions and may be supported across different fields and contexts. For example, within the sociology of scientific knowledge, epistemic relativism underscores the relativising impact of social factors on the formation of scientific beliefs.

Paul Boghossian has launched one of the fiercest attacks on epistemic relativism in recent years. He defines epistemic relativism in three theses (Boghossian 2006: 73): (A) There are no absolute epistemic facts ('Epistemic non-absolutism'); (B) Epistemic judgements of the form 'Y justifies belief X' must be replaced by the qualified judgement 'According to the epistemic system E, Y justifies belief X' ('Epistemic relationism'); and (C) There are many different, genuinely alternative epistemic systems ('Epistemic pluralism'). Boghossian's critique of epistemic relativism as an incoherent stance has sparked extensive debate and attracted sharp critical remarks from relativists (MacFarlane 2008; Kusch 2020b: 7–10). Although this Element primarily focuses on alethic relativism, we will explore in Sections 4 and 5 that epistemic relativism holds profound implications for the concept of traditional monotheism.

Moral relativism: Broadly speaking, moral relativism encompasses views that regard claims in the domain of morality – judgements on what is right or wrong, just or unjust, good or evil – as not true objectively, but only relatively. Moral relativists typically deny the existence of objective morality independent of our epistemic access. Along these lines, the truth of moral judgements is deemed relative to, and dependent upon, various cultural, historical, religious, and individual frameworks. As these frameworks determine what is considered right or wrong and good or evil, there exists a plurality of moral claims that are relatively true. In terms of their status (being relatively true), these claims must be deemed equally valid, although some relativists – as indicated previously – dispute this. Three different types of moral relativism are customarily distinguished in the discussion (Moser & Carson 2001; Westacott 2024): First, *descriptive* moral relativism, based on the empirical fact that there are culturally irreconcilable differences in ethical norms and values, often stemming from incompatible moral frameworks in different epochs, cultures, societies, and religions. Second, *metaethical* relativism is a theory about the nature of morality that assumes the nonexistence of moral absolutes. Third, *normative* moral relativism is a prescriptive doctrine that deems it wrong or intolerant to stipulate one's own moral views and norms regarding other moral beliefs, as all beliefs are seen as relative and embedded in a respective culture, society, religion, and so forth. Relativist conceptions of morality have serious implications for monotheism. After examining the basic principles of monotheism, we will address a major challenge of moral relativism in Section 5.

3 Approaches to Monotheistic Relativism

The last section provided an introduction to the basic idea of relativism and to some essential distinctions related to it. In this section, we explore two approaches to religious relativism. What are the core ideas of religious relativism? This version of relativism broadly assumes that beliefs about faith matters are only relatively true, depending on particular frameworks of religious systems, communities, doctrines, or believers. The underlying idea is that a religious belief can be true relative to a religious framework Y and, simultaneously, false relative to a different religious framework Z. As there exist no nonrelative or absolute standards for judging if a religious framework is true (or false) objectively, all religious beliefs are of equal validity. In this relativist sense, religious beliefs are true only in dependence on specific religious belief systems (Meister 2006: 33). Furthermore, religious relativists frequently suggest that adherence to such systems and religious communities is hardly determined by rational reasoning or weighing of the advantages and disadvantages of particular religions, but is rather conditioned by the coincidence of the geographical, cultural, or social origin of the religious individual.

Regarding religious relativism, this section discusses the approaches of Joseph Runzo and James K. A. Smith, which originate from the context of monotheism or are closely related to it. Importantly, both explicitly label their concept as 'relativism'. Within the spectrum of monotheism, one can find positions that employ an unspecific, non-philosophical concept of relativism (Wilfred 2006). Other positions do not explicitly identify as 'relativism' or even deny this classification, yet can still be interpreted as such. For example, the postmodern thought of Italian philosopher Gianni Vattimo, who frequently adopted and modified Christian themes, might fall into this category, particularly with his thesis that 'only a relativistic God can save us' (Vattimo 2011: 47). Due to space constraints, we focus on the explicit religious relativism in Runzo and Smith.

Two aspects should be noted in advance. First, we will not examine possible versions of religious relativism that do not stem from or are not somehow related to the monotheistic traditions – a possible example of this could be the Jain doctrine of relativity or 'many-sidedness' (*anekāntavāda*), although it is unclear whether this view even amounts to a genuine relativist position (Webb 2023) – simply because the subject matter of this Cambridge Elements Series is 'Religion and Monotheism'. Second, both approaches to monotheistic relativism originate solely from the context of Christianity. What about relativistic currents in other monotheistic traditions, such as Judaism, Islam, or in some streams of Hinduism? Despite careful research and investigation, I have not become aware of any distinctive relativist approach in non-Christian monotheism that would even come close to what is philosophically termed 'relativism', as explored in the previous section. Presumably, these non-Christian monotheistic traditions have not been inclined towards relativism in their doctrine or have not yet reflected on the possible implications of the Western idea of relativism. As we will see in Section 4.3, they also appear not to have developed any conceptions of anti-relativism. For clarity, I am not suggesting that non-Christian monotheistic traditions have never, in the broadest sense, entertained any unspecified relativist ideas or thoughts. However, I assume that no comprehensive approaches have yet been formulated within these traditions that explicitly claim to be relativist or could be labelled 'relativism' from a philosophical perspective.

3.1 Analytic Monotheistic Relativism: Joseph Runzo

In the wake of renewed philosophical interest in relativism during the 1970s, Joseph Runzo, an American Professor of Philosophy of Religion, was among the first scholars in religious studies to develop an explicit version of religious relativism. He introduced his approach most notably in his 1986 book *Reason, Relativism and God* (Runzo 1986). Since then, he has written several articles on the topic that refined and specified his position, particularly regarding the potential of relativism to balance the challenges of religious diversity (Runzo 2008; Runzo 2011).

Runzo has consistently argued since the 1980s that we are living in 'an age of relativism' (Runzo 1986: 4). He bases his diagnosis on the emerging general public awareness that each belief or truth claim, whether religious or secular, is historically conditioned and hence relative to cultural, social, political, or religious factors. In such a relativistic age, it has become evident for Runzo, concerning the huge diversity of religions, that belonging to a religious community and believing certain religious doctrines is not a matter of rational and balanced consideration, after weighing up truth claims of various options, but largely 'an accident of birth' (Runzo 2011: 61; see also Runzo 2008: 64). Unfortunately, Runzo does not cite any empirical studies or surveys as a corroboration for his diagnosis. In contrast, one could object that prevalent debates in politics, society, and religions give evidence that contentious issues about truth and morality do not appear to be regarded as relative to the opposing parties.

Runzo refers to insights from the social sciences, especially from the sociology of knowledge – he mentions the famous theorists Thomas Kuhn, Peter Berger, and Thomas Luckmann – which have shown him that reality is constructed and that purportedly objective scientific facts are essentially 'only paradigm-related facts' (Runzo 1986: 7). The sociology of knowledge – notable proponents such as David Bloor and Martin Kusch have already been mentioned – examines how human thought is shaped by its social context and explores the influence of dominant ideas on societies. With its various schools and currents, the sociology of knowledge represents a controversial theory that we cannot delve into further here (for a critical discussion, see Trigg 2001). Runzo derives from Kuhn, Berger, and Luckmann that all our experiences and truth claims, whether religious or not, stem from and are structured by specific worldviews. For him, conflicts between religions should be perceived as conflicts between different religious truth claims, which in turn derive from '*essentially* different' and incompatible worldviews (Runzo 2008: 62). Against that background, Runzo's relativist construal strives to explore whether absolutism in monotheistic faith is compatible with his view that truth is relative in contemporary culture (Runzo 1986: 4, 13, 17; Runzo 2008: 61). In this line of argument, Runzo extols his conception of religious relativism as the only account capable of reconciling the two poles. Moreover, he also prompts Christians 'to move toward a Christian Relativism' (Runzo 2008: 75).

Three aspects are worth mentioning at this point. First, in terms of content, Runzo's approach is devised on the basis of the Christian worldview. He defends what he calls '*theological relativism*' (Runzo 1986: xiii), a position he views as capable of demonstrating the compatibility between absolute theological truth claims and a relativist epistemology. Second, regarding methodology, Runzo situates his religious relativism within the framework of analytic philosophy, which he deems the most promising resource for his project (Runzo 1986: xv). Third, concerning the sources of influence, he traces the emergence of religious relativism back to sceptical attitudes towards religious authority and dogma in the historical context of the sixteenth-century Reformation. From Runzo's viewpoint, this sceptical tendency was particularly received and elaborated by Immanuel Kant, especially in his critical reflections on religion and in his famous distinction between 'phenomena' (things as they appear to human cognition) and 'noumena' (things as they are in themselves). For Runzo, the resulting Kantian notion – that knowledge of God is always only the knowledge of God as he appears according to our epistemic faculties, and thus not as he is in himself – was a significant step towards theological relativism (Runzo 1986: 9). According to his interpretation of Kant, monotheistic truth claims are relative to how individual believers or communities conceive of the noumenal God. Runzo is particularly influenced by John Hick's pluralist construal of the Kantian distinction between 'noumena' and 'phenomena' (Hick 2004: xxii). With his religious relativism, Runzo intends to draw on Hick's religious pluralism, but at the same time to overcome its shortcomings and deficiencies.[6] Accordingly, the occurrence of various religions is meant to be the outcome of different legitimate and relatively true conceptualisations of the noumenal divine reality. Religious adherents experience this ultimate reality in various interpretations and conceptions of the divine. As there is no access to the noumenal divine independent of our worldviews, the non-epistemic or realist idea of objective and universal religious truth seems to be unfounded and pointless for Runzo. In this respect, he regards his relativist approach as grounded in an '*idealist epistemology*' in the lineage of Kant (Runzo 2008: 66).

---

[6] As further precursors of theistic relativism, Runzo identifies theologians Friedrich Schleiermacher, Ernst Troeltsch, and Rudolf Bultmann, along with philosopher Ludwig Wittgenstein.

What are the basic tenets of Runzo's relativism? He formulates two principles (Runzo 2008: 12–13). The first is called '*Diversity principle of religious
relativism*' and refers to the globally recognisable fact of religious plurality.
Since religions are, in Runzo's view, social constructs, developed within
different cultures or historical periods, they often prove incompatible in
terms of doctrine or core beliefs. The second is called '*Dependency principle
of religious relativism*' and reads as follows: 'For any religious belief, *P*,
professed within a religious community, *R*, if *P* expresses a true statement
within *R*, then the truth of that statement depends, at least in part, on the
pattern of thought of *R*.' This 'principle' largely reflects what we have already
outlined as relationship of dependency, a key feature of relativism. The
ambiguous proviso 'at least in part' is not elucidated by Runzo. It might
imply that his account allows exceptions of objective truth and does not
necessarily represent a version of normative relativism. However, this interpretation would be incorrect, as the context of the quote and other passages
demonstrate. Runzo clearly defends a version of normative relativism. In his
view, the truth of propositions 'is not just in fact, but must be, societally
relative', as 'truth is necessarily relative to different enculturated patterns of
thought' (Runzo 1986: 13; Runzo 2008: 67).

Following these preliminary remarks, Runzo defines his notion of religious
relativism as follows: 'At least one world religion is correct, and the truth of any
religion's truth claims is relative to the worldview(s) of its community of
adherents' (Runzo 2011: 65; see also Runzo 2008: 63). It is striking that
Runzo speaks not only of 'truth', but also of 'correctness'. However, he does
not provide further information on what he means by 'correctness' and whether
he associates it with a semantic difference from 'truth'. Religions may be
'correct' in many ways, for example, if they follow closely the teachings of
their founder. If all adherents were supportive of this practice, that religion
might be termed 'correct', namely, 'relative to the worldview(s) of its community of adherents'. In this scenario, the assessment of correctness would be an
internal decision made by the respective followers. Regardless of whether such
an epistemic construal of 'correctness' is meaningful, the consideration of
a religion's objective and non-epistemic truth addresses a distinct matter. As
indicated previously, non-epistemic or realist notions of truth typically posit
a mind-independent reality that renders metaphysical or scientific truth claims
objectively true (or false), even if we cannot fully ascertain or conclusively
corroborate these claims. For epistemic or anti-realist notions of truth, it is not
a mind-independent reality but rather a process of justification that renders
a truth claim true. A claim is considered true if someone has reasonable or
justifiable grounds for holding it to be true.

In this context, one might ask in what sense a religion can be 'true' in Runzo's framework. Is the belief 'There is a transcendent God' true in a non-epistemic sense, insofar as what it claims actually obtains – that God exists as a mind-independent reality – even if we are unable to conclusively verify it? Or is it true in an epistemic sense, because the community of adherents deems itself justified in believing it to be true? Remarkably, Runzo's '*idealist epistemology*' is inclined to an epistemic notion of truth, in which what counts as truth is determined by internal decision and justification within a specific religious worldview. He describes this idealism as follows: 'the world we experience and understand is not the world independent of our perceiving but a world at least in part structured by our minds' (Runzo 2008: 66). At this point, Runzo also leaves open what he exactly means by his proviso 'at least in parts'. He may be referring to a non-idealistic element of his idealism – the claim that a mind-independent reality of a noumenal God exists. The ambiguity might conceal a Kantian problem for Runzo: If all religious experience is mind-dependent and relative to specific worldviews, how can we ascertain the mind-independent fact of a noumenal divine reality? According to Kant, the idea of *noumena* expresses no more than a limiting concept, insofar as *noumena* are, by definition, unknowable. However, the context of the passage makes it evident that Runzo is not aiming to compromise his epistemic epistemology.

In light of the aforementioned remarks, the substitution of 'correctness' for 'truth' in Runzo's definition of religious relativism may no longer be surprising. While from a realist perspective only one (or no) religion can be true – provided they are ultimately different and incompatible with each other – from Runzo's both anti-realist and relativist viewpoint, several religions may simultaneously be equally 'true', 'valid', 'adequate', or 'correct', relative to the specific worldview of their community of adherents. In line with this relativistic reasoning, Runzo concludes that 'different religions have different constitutive sets of core truth-claims, and that – while these sets of core truth claims are mutually incompatible – each set of truth-claims is probably adequate in itself' (Runzo 2008: 71).

What does this suggest about Runzo's view on the relationship between monotheism and relativism? For Runzo, monotheistic truth claims describe and delimit God as experienced and theologically interpreted by monotheists, based on their specific worldview. In addition, there are also 'true', 'valid', 'adequate', and 'correct' religious experiences and descriptions of this noumenal divine reality within '*contrasting*' theologies (Runzo 2008: 71). The significance of this perspective becomes apparent when comparing it with a polytheistic concept of multiple deities. Even if this doctrine contradicts the central monotheistic claim that only one supreme God exists, according to

Runzo's relativism, both religious views could still be considered 'true', 'correct', and 'adequate in itself'.

It becomes evident that Runzo's commitment to an epistemic conception of truth, while dismissing non-epistemic notions, comes at a significant cost. His relativist stance presents several challenges, including the difficulty of establishing criteria for rationally evaluating religious claims as true or false. According to the principle of non-contradiction, only one religious doctrine in our example can be true – either the monotheistic or the polytheistic one. Of course, both doctrines could simultaneously be 'adequate' or 'correct' in a certain sense, but not true. The epistemic limitation that finite beings can never definitely ascertain the truth of religious teachings does not absolve theology and philosophy from the rational pursuit of truth in answering the metaphysical question of whether only one God exists, multiple deities, or none at all. Runzo's approach does not provide external or worldview-independent criteria as arbiters for determining religious truth, but relies solely on internal criteria. Therefore, it is exclusively within each religious community that the truth or correctness of its own faith is established, based on its particular worldview. However, one might question how likely it is for a religious community to conclude that central truth claims of its own belief system are 'false' or 'incorrect', especially when external criteria, such as the law of non-contradiction, might be dismissed as, for instance, a purely Western concept? Generally, it appears difficult or even impossible to dispute the truth of a religious doctrine that includes bizarre ideas of the divine or advocates for inhumane practices without external criteria, particularly when its proponents believe themselves fully justified in holding it true. A religious community could easily dismiss external theological enquiries, proposals, or criticisms as irrelevant or pointless, arguing that they are based on an '*essentially* different' worldview. Overall, according to Runzo's approach, it appears that religious adherents are somehow trapped within the confines of their geographically or culturally acquired perspective.

As previously stated, the central concern of Runzo's relativism aims to demonstrate the compatibility of the 'absoluteness' of core statements of monotheism and the 'relativity of truth' (Runzo 1986: 4). While we have investigated what Runzo means by 'relativity of truth', it has remained unclear what he exactly associates with 'absoluteness'. Runzo identifies two senses in which religious truths can be absolute: an 'epistemological' and a 'psychological' sense (Runzo 1986: 220). Concerning the first sense, Runzo suggests that 'an 'absolute truth' is true in every possible world conceivable by *every* possible conceiver' (Runzo 1986: 44). However, can such absolute truths indeed exist within Runzo's framework of relativism? Surprisingly, the answer is affirmative. As examples of such absolute truths, Runzo refers to 'propositions which are essential for rationality' (Runzo 1986: 220), such as the law of non-contradiction. According to his reasoning, the 'epistemological' absoluteness of rational principles goes beyond all patterns of thought, conceptual schemes, or worldviews. Runzo asserts that there are rational 'meta-criteria', such as coherence and thoroughness, that can be applied across worldviews to assess the acceptability of each viewpoint (Runzo 2008: 74; Runzo 2011: 71). In this context, his recourse to absolute truths appears to be a strategic response to the problem of external criteria previously mentioned. However, it is questionable whether Runzo's recourse can be successful, based on his relativistic stance. One might object that his relativism, characterised by the 'Plurality' and 'Dependency' principles, does not possess the necessary conceptual resources to account for such absolute truths and worldview-independent meta-criteria. For instance, how might Runzo respond to the allegation that his relativism adheres to a colonialist and Western understanding of rationality, which does not apply to Chinese conceptions of reasoning? If truth, as already quoted, is 'necessarily relative to different enculturated patterns of thought', it seems inconsistent to claim at the same time the existence of absolute truths *beyond* these enculturated patterns. Logically, the situation presents a dichotomy at this point: either all truths are worldview-relative, or they are not. If the former were true, there simply could not be any worldview-independent truths. If the latter were true, and some truths were worldview-independent while others were not, it would lead to a regress problem regarding whether the criteria used to distinguish worldview-dependent truths from worldview-independent truths are themselves worldview-independent.

Concerning the second, 'psychological', sense in which religious truths can be absolute, Runzo refers to the state of commitment and confidence a person holds in the truth of a belief. Some religious beliefs, according to Runzo, are held with an 'absolute' conviction and commitment. Moreover, it is possible for him to believe that absolute truths exist in a 'psychological' sense, 'which are *not* epistemologically absolute, but which the person holding them would be irrational not to treat as epistemologically absolute' (Runzo 1986: 221). At least two points are problematic in his considerations. First, Runzo ignores the commonly used distinction in philosophy between a proposition and the propositional attitude towards that proposition (for instance, one can believe, doubt, or deny it in various cognitive degrees or forms of commitment). Evidently, the propositional attitude of being 'absolutely' committed to a belief or proposition has nothing to do with the question of whether this belief is true or false. Consequently, Runzo's 'psychological' sense of absoluteness appears to be outside the semantic spectrum that is generally associated with the term 'absolute' in philosophy and theology.

Second, Runzo seems to have a peculiar understanding of rationality with regard to the 'psychological' sense of absoluteness. How rational might it be to be 'absolutely' committed, in a 'psychological' sense, to the truth of a religious belief, when one knows that it is simply false in an 'epistemological' sense? Such an attitude appears less rational than fideistic, which, roughly, describes a religious view that doubts or denies the importance of rationality for the justification of its truth claims – certainly a position that Runzo does not want to defend.

Due to space limitations, we must conclude our critical discussion of Runzo's relativism, even though some aspects remain unexplored. It is useful to briefly connect the analysis of his position with our introduction to relativism in the last section. All four features of normative relativism are present in Runzo's approach. In short, he asserts, first, the *dependency* of religious beliefs on worldviews; second, that his relativism is capable of *conflict resolution* in the context of interfaith disagreements; third, the feature of *non-absolutism*, insofar as no worldview-independent standards exist for assessing a belief as true objectively; and fourth, the *equal validity* of religious truth claims, as they all are both true relatively and 'adequate in itself'. Does his approach ultimately succeed in demonstrating that his version of religious relativism is compatible with the core ideas of monotheism? As long as we have not yet examined the concept of monotheism and its connection to absolutism, it seems advisable to refrain from drawing final conclusions at this point. However, as the previous analysis has indicated, several deficiencies in Runzo's approach render the compatibility he asserts somewhat dubious. Therefore, Christians should be cautious in following his advice 'to move toward a Christian Relativism'.

3.2 Pragmatic Monotheistic Relativism: James K. A. Smith

The second proponent of monotheistic relativism, James K. A. Smith, has elaborated his position in the philosophical tradition of pragmatism. Pragmatism has emerged as a reform of philosophy in the second half of the nineteenth century in the United States, particularly around the philosophers Charles Sanders Pierce and William James, and has since developed into two main strands, based on their respective approaches (Misak 2013). In broad terms, pragmatism assumes that the meaning of philosophical categories or concepts, such as 'truth', should not be determined primarily by theoretical considerations but rather by their practical applications and consequences within a particular community.

Smith is professor of philosophy at Calvin University in Michigan, where he holds a chair in Applied Reformed Theology. In our context, he may have become known for his book *Who's Afraid of Relativism? Community,*

Contingency, and Creaturehood (Smith 2014a). Smith presents himself as both a conservative Christian and an intellectual dissenter or non-conformist. He strives to rehabilitate philosophical authors or ideas that have hitherto been spurned or disdained from a Christian perspective, by emphasising their (allegedly) true significance for traditional monotheistic faith. In a previous book, Smith used insights from the 'unholy trinity' of Jacques Derrida, Jean-François Lyotard, and Michel Foucault to formulate a version of Christian postmodernism (Smith 2006). His book on relativism is intended as an extension of this project, attempting to dispel the fear of relativism and focussing on the pragmatist insights of Ludwig Wittgenstein, Richard Rorty, and Robert Brandom. Essentially, Smith's analysis of the three philosophers aims to outline a position of Christian relativism within the framework of pragmatism. As the subtitle of the book indicates, his approach is concerned with the idea of contingency, which, in his opinion, is marginalised or even suppressed in Christian absolutism and only preserved in a pragmatist relativism. Remarkably, Smith pledges that his account does not lead to an 'eviscerated, liberal Christianity', but to a 'more orthodox Christian faith' and a 'catholic conservatism' (Smith 2014a: 18). Similar to Runzo, he is firmly convinced 'that Christians *should* be 'relativists', of a sort, precisely because of the biblical understanding of creation and creaturehood' (Smith 2014a: 12). For the sake of simplicity, my analysis is confined to Smith's interpretation of Rorty, which forms the core of his relativist position. We trace his line of thought in four steps.

1. As the starting point of his approach, Smith fiercely criticises what he perceives as a traditional Christian consensus on truth absolutism. Within this consensus, it is undisputed that the Christian message proclaims absolute truth, and that truth absolutism is 'the very antithesis of relativism' (Smith 2014a: 16). In stark contrast to that consensus, Smith argues that truth absolutism, from an orthodox Christian vantage point, is 'heretical', because it implies 'an evasion of contingency and a suppression of creaturehood' (Smith 2014a: 16). He even goes so far as to assert that truth absolutism is 'at the heart of the first sin in the garden' (Smith 2014a: 30). Smith is serious about this thesis, as he associates it with a theological narrative, the first part of which can be summarised as follows (Smith 2014a: 29–31, 35–36, 111–114): From a Christian perspective, we are finite social beings, created by God. As such, our existence and knowledge are always contingent and relative to God. Hence, we are not capable of holding absolute truths. Our knowledge of reality is always relative to the social practices of our respective community. We can never know whether our beliefs correspond to reality, because there is no epistemic access to such community-independent knowledge. Everything created is relative to God. Even the truth of

the Christian faith is relative to God's revelation. In contrast, the assertion that we can know absolute or objective truths denies our contingency and yields 'a God-like picture of human reason' (Smith 2014a: 35). 'Objectivity', in this sense, is a liberal idea, bequeathed to us by the Enlightenment. Therefore, an appropriate orthodox understanding of the Christian faith necessitates a relativist notion of truth.

Smith makes derisive comments in his book about what he sees as misunderstanding, distortion, or even stupidity of the critics of relativism and pragmatism. Conversely, critics of his approach may object that his portrayal of truth absolutism amounts to a caricature. First, Smith is certainly right when he underscores the importance of creaturehood and contingency for Christianity. However, associating an appropriate understanding of these biblical teachings solely with truth relativism seems implausible. Second, throughout his book, Smith neither presents any references to current debates on relativism nor provides a precise philosophical definition of 'relativism'. This may explain that he often unknowingly conflates relativism with relationalism, a theoretical position, previously mentioned, that solely underlines the relational nature of entities. For instance, Smith's thesis that everything created is relative to God does not necessarily imply relativism and may also be defended by an absolutist. Third, Smith's allegation that an absolutist strives to 'achieve Godlike knowledge' (Smith 2014a: 109) or even pretends to be 'godlike insofar as she *doesn't seem to depend on anyone*' (Smith 2014a: 99) is simply incorrect. It remains a philosophical misconception to assume that positions of truth absolutism necessarily entail something like a 'God's eye view'. Smith's relativism is inclined to an epistemic notion of truth (even if he does not use the term) and repudiates the non-epistemic idea of absolute or objective truths. As noted earlier, realist conceptions typically assert that there can be objective truths, which are true if that what they claim really obtains, independently of whether we can sufficiently justify or verify them. Yet, they usually ascribe only *perspectival*, and not divine or meta-perspectival, knowledge to their position. Moreover, they require claimants to substantiate and justify their truth claims in epistemic terms as far as possible. Of course, all claims to truth can turn out to be false. Overall, the attribution of 'Godlike knowledge' appears to be a misleading but not uncommon strategy to cast non-epistemic or realist conceptions of truth in an unfavourable light. In this respect, the more general criticism that Smith conflates the concepts of truth and justification (Echeverria 2014: 267; a rejoinder in Smith 2014b) seems warranted.

2. The following part of Smith's narrative focuses on relativism as the antidote to truth absolutism. Since 'relativism' is only a vague term for Smith, encompassing various perspectives, he singles out Richard Rorty's relativist

approach as a model for his further analysis. As the reason for this choice, Smith points out that Rorty is constantly decried by 'middlebrow Christian intellectuals and analytic philosophers' as a relativist (Smith 2014a: 17). In other words, Smith refrains from elaborating on the concept of relativism and begins his examination directly with an approach labelled as 'relativism' in some circles. He takes this further by asserting that since Rorty's position is mainly ascribed to pragmatism in contemporary philosophy, it is appropriate to identify the entire tradition of pragmatism as relativistic (Smith 2014a: 17–19). This line of reasoning raises various questions. First, is it legitimate to equate pragmatism with relativism? Certainly, convergences between both theories exist and pragmatism is frequently referred to as a version of relativism. However, even though pragmatists typically reject truth absolutism and often point to the diversity of social contexts to determine the meaning of concepts and perspectives, compelling reasons have been presented for not simply equating the two doctrines (Boncompagni 2020: 131). Second, is Rorty genuinely a relativist? In philosophy, there has been a broad discussion on this matter. Rorty was dissatisfied with that label, as with any '-ism', and instead preferred the term 'ethnocentrism' for his position. With recourse to our definition in Section 2, it would be overreaching to categorise his often ambiguous or ironic ideas as a version of normative relativism. Yet, based on a broader concept of relativism, it can be argued that some of Rorty's views are relativistic or inclined towards relativism. However, such an interpretation requires at least a specific concept of relativism, which Smith does not offer. Third, how is Rorty's relativism, in contrast to truth absolutism, supposed to provide insight into an adequate understanding of the monotheistic teachings of creation and contingency? Smith's response is outlined in the third part of his narrative.

3. His reading of Rorty goes something like this (Smith 2014a: 73–114): In his book *Philosophy and the Mirror of Nature*, Rorty successfully dismantles the traditional concept of representationalism. This concept relies on the idea – primarily developed by René Descartes – that our knowledge can, in a certain way, correctly mirror or represent the external world. According to Rorty, representationalists naively assume the existence of an internal space filled with mental ideas and representations, which are supposed to somehow copy or mirror the external world as it truly is. For Smith, who follows Rorty in this criticism, this view of knowledge is misguided for several reasons, especially because it 'forgets its own contingency' (Smith 2014a: 81). Due to their epistemic limitations, human beings are incapable of recognising something like objective truth as correspondence between beliefs in the mind and the external world. In contrast, the acquisition of knowledge should be understood in terms of social practice. To this extent, for Smith, beliefs must primarily be

seen as a form of 'know-how', acquired, examined, and justified in a process of interaction among members of a specific community. Against that backdrop, the idea of truth should not be associated with a correspondence relation, but rather with the pragmatic notion of what is good or beneficial for a particular community to deem true. Smith repeatedly cites Rorty's provocative statement that truth is nothing more than 'what our peers will, *ceteris paribus*, let us get away with saying' (Rorty 1979: 176; Smith 2014a: 84). In Smith's words: 'Knowledge is a social, cultural *accomplishment*, which means that what *counts* as knowledge is inextricably linked to social life – to that infamous "circle of our peers"' (Smith 2014a: 89). In this line of Smith's thought, the idea of truth turns out to be relative to, and dependent upon, a respective community of practice (Smith 2014a: 87, 98, 167). The claim is that Rorty's relativist approach exposes the foundations of the contingency of knowledge and the creational dependence on communities of practice, 'who gift us with a world of meaning' (Smith 2014a: 115). Smith's concludes that 'Representationalism denies our dependence' (Smith 2014a: 101). Conversely, any attempt to refute 'the pragmatist account of meaning and knowledge amounts to denying the finite, creaturely conditions of human knowledge' (Smith 2014a: 107). For reasons of space, we must leave open questions about the plausibility of Smith's interpretation of Rorty and the allegations against representationalism. Instead, we will focus on what Christianity can learn from Rorty's pragmatic relativism, according to Smith's perspective.

4. Supplemented by interpretations of Wittgenstein, Brandom, and the Lutheran theologian George Lindbeck, Smith assumes that Christianity must be understood as a form of life, characterised by a network of communal religious practices from which the meaning of faith primarily emerges. Believing rather implies a knowing-*how* than a knowing-*that*, as 'our *doings* precede our *thinkings*' (Smith 2014a: 160). In this regard, Christian doctrine is relative to its community of religious practice. In other words, the assertion that Christ is the Lord holds true within the confines of Christian practice (Smith 2014a: 167–169). Since Christians, like all people, do not possess knowledge that extends beyond their communal practices, they can only claim relative truth for their teachings and should refrain from asserting an absolute standpoint. According to Smith, relativism is the only approach that adequately comprehends the Christian doctrines of contingency and creaturehood. Only relativist pragmatism teaches us to renounce the 'idolatrous hubris' of claiming absolute truth (Smith 2014a: 180) and to recognise our own dependence on God.

The previous reconstruction of Smith's narrative should be sufficient to grasp the basic tenets of his religious relativism. Smith is certainly successful in his endeavour to challenge and reconsider traditional views and doctrines of

Christianity. However, in light of our definition of relativism and the four features specified, making sense of his relativist ideas has been somewhat challenging. At times, his statements oscillate between descriptive and normative relativism. The fundamental problem in interpreting Smith's approach lies in his reluctance to articulate a precise philosophical concept of relativism. His reference to pragmatist positions that do not consider themselves relativistic, but which he, lacking a clear concept, labels as such, exacerbates the problem. In a footnote, Smith indeed raises the objection of whether Rorty is the right collaborator to promote a conservative understanding of Christianity and its teachings of contingency and creation (Smith 2014a: 74). As Smith also lacks reliable definitions of the terms 'contingency' and 'creation', he easily dismisses this objection and incorporates Rorty's position into his narrative of heretical truth absolutism and salvific relativism. To this effect, the provocative colouring of many of his statements often paints a hardly convincing black-and-white picture of the debate on relativism, thereby impeding a serious reception of his views. Finally, the crucial question remains whether Christians should indeed become relativists, as Smith urges at the beginning of his book. Although we have not yet examined the concept of monotheism, there are compelling reasons for Christians to resist this allurement. Despite the irony of Rorty and Smith, truth should not be what Christian peers will let believers get away with saying.

4 Monotheism, Absolutism, and Anti-Relativism

After providing an overview of relativism and two relativist approaches within the monotheistic tradition, we now turn to traditional monotheism and its concept of a single supreme God to establish a basis for analysing its relationship to relativism. This section first introduces key aspects of the monotheistic concept of God as it initially emerged in Judaism, before being adopted and transformed by Christianity, and subsequently by Islam. Afterwards, it explores the significance of revelation and truth in monotheistic theologies. Finally, the section examines whether certain forms of anti-relativism have already been developed and discussed in the traditions of Judaism, Christianity, and Islam.

In the course of the section, three pivotal aspects of Abrahamic monotheism are identified and discussed to clarify our topic. First, *theological absolutism* posits that God is a supreme transcendent being and an absolute reality, independent of the material universe and human conception. Second, *redemptive universalism* refers to God's intention to redeem all people, thereby encouraging the missionary propagation of faith beyond the confines of one's own monotheistic tradition. Third, *truth-objectivism* asserts that the revelation of the monotheistic God includes a cognitive dimension and embodies an objective, non-epistemic notion of the manifested truth.

4.1 The Idea of God

Monotheism encompasses views that assume the existence of a single supreme and transcendent deity, most commonly revered and worshipped as 'God'. In general, adherents of the Abrahamic religions of Judaism, Christianity, and Islam conceive of God as a unique, benevolent, and morally perfect being, who created the world out of free will and, in his loving dedication, continues to sustain and intervene in it to guide and redeem all humankind. Monotheism differs from polytheism, the belief in the existence of multiple deities or divine spirits, and from henotheism, the belief that there is a single, supreme deity that must be venerated, without denying the existence of other, usually inferior deities. Judaism, Christianity, and Islam are monotheistic religions with common theological origins in what they understand as the revelation of God. Yet, monotheistic notions and features also characterise several other religious traditions such as the Bahá'í Faith, Sikhism, Zoroastrianism, and Yazidism. Within Hinduism, monotheistic currents and schools predate the influence of Judaism and Christianity, such as Shaivism, in which the deity of Śhiva is worshipped as the supreme being.

In the following discussion, we will focus solely on the monotheism of the three Abrahamic religions for two reasons. On the one hand, the majority of monotheistic traditions in other religions, particularly within Hinduism (Flood 2020: 7–10), differs significantly from Abrahamic monotheism. For instance, while God is perceived as the ultimate reality in almost all monotheistic traditions, some currents of non-Abrahamic monotheism subscribe to an ontological monism, merging or identifying divine reality with the reality of the phenomenal world (such as the *Advaita Vedanta* school in Hinduism). This distinguishes them from Judaism, Christianity, and Islam, which clearly differentiate between the ultimate reality of the creator and the reality of his creation, emphasising an ontological dualism. On the other hand, many non-Abrahamic monotheistic traditions represent more a form of orthopraxy, primarily relying on rituals and rules, than orthodoxy, which in Judaism, Christianity, and Islam, places a strong emphasis on doctrinal matters and theology (Flood 2020: 1).

At this point, it is essential to abandon the idea that Abrahamic monotheism represents a somehow homogeneous or uniform religious tradition, compared to the variety and diversity of other religions. Evidently, there are too many profound differences between Judaism, Christianity, and Islam in terms of doctrine, ritual, ethics, and practices. However, despite these differences, I posit that there are fundamental accordances or convergences among them, particularly regarding their shared roots in the Hebrew tradition. Most importantly, from this specific origin, the distinct monotheistic idea of a single supreme and benevolent God – who reveals himself to his people and is alone worthy of worship – gradually emerged. It was solely through various attempts to comprehend this unique idea in faith and reconstruct it theologically that the Abrahamic religions diversified across different historical contexts.

To better understand the concept of God in these three religions, we briefly examine the origin and historical development of monotheism in the Semitic world of the first millennium BC. Although monotheistic ideas may have initially arisen in Mesopotamian religions and particularly in Egypt under Pharaoh Akhenaten, Judaism is commonly considered the most ancient monotheistic religion. In theology, it is recognised that biblical monotheism in Israelite-Jewish religious history emerged very late. This development followed polytheistic and henotheistic phases, and was precipitated by incisive historical events for the people of Israel, especially the destruction of Jerusalem and the First Temple by the Babylonians in 587 BC and the subsequent exile. Recent research has suggested that the biblical God was originally a desert war god from the south, probably between Negev and Egypt, before gradually becoming the adopted God of Israel under the predominant theonym YHWH, as recorded in the Book of Exodus (Römer 2015: 1–4, 242–253; Soskice 2023: 16–23). It took considerable time, marked by several significant historical events, for this desert god to become the sole and transcendent deity of Judaism around 400–300 BC. Later, in different historical and theological contexts, he arose as the supreme God in Christianity and subsequently in Islam.

What historical circumstances enabled YHWH to become the only God of Israel? Due to space limitations, we need to focus on the crucial period following the destruction of Jerusalem. Biblical research has indicated that this upheaval and the subsequent deportation of large parts of the Judean elite were understood as a catastrophe and provoked a major theological crisis concerning the legitimacy of belief in the power of YHWH. Correspondingly, destructive explanations for this catastrophe would have been plausible: either the gods of Babylon are simply stronger than YHWH, or he has abandoned his people (Römer 2015: 214). However, the emergence of theological absolutism within Judaism was the result of unexpected constructive explanations of this historical turning point, two of which are particularly noteworthy.

The first originated from the Deuteronomistic school, which presumably comprised mostly descendants of scribes at the Judean court. Within a theological framework, they reconstructed the previous history of Israel, starting from Moses up to the subversion of Jerusalem, as a continuous and coherent plan of God. Consequently, the Babylonian invasion and the destruction of the Temple were seen as God's own will, by which he intended to punish the people of Israel for worshipping foreign gods: 'Indeed, Jerusalem and Judah so angered the Lord that he expelled them from his presence' (2 Kings 24:20). The second narrative came from the Priestly tradition, probably a group of priests closely associated with the Temple cult before the deportation. Their reconstruction of Israel's history began much earlier than that of the Deuteronomistic school, starting with the creation of the world and humanity by God. The Priestly source thus promoted a rather strong inclusive and universal monotheism, as the God of Israel is described as the cosmic creator of all human beings, who is abundantly powerful and governs history. Furthermore, for the Priestly authors, all peoples who believe in any deity in fact worship the transcendent God of Israel, even if they do not recognise his true identity (Römer 2015: 226, 252). Similar to the Deuteronomistic school, the Babylonian exile is viewed as God's judgement, for which he utilised the Babylonians and later the Persians as instruments of history.

In summary, biblical research has illustrated that both narratives marked a 'theological revolution' (Römer 2015: 220) that firmly paved the way for monotheism and its belief in a transcendent and universal God. According to this revolutionary idea, God is completely distinct from the false deities of other peoples, who are impotent and anthropomorphic: 'Why should the nations say, 'Where is their God?' Our God is in the heavens; he does whatever he pleases. Their idols are silver and gold, the work of human hands' (Psalm 113). The God YHWH simultaneously became the particular deity of the people of Israel and the supreme God of the entire universe and all peoples of the earth. Accordingly, Jewish Monotheism has both an *inclusivist*, universal alignment, as God is considered to be the supreme deity for all humankind, and an *exclusivist*, particularistic alignment (Römer 2015: 231–232), as it was specifically the people of Israel whom he had chosen, as 'a light to the nations' (Isaiah 49:6), for his covenant with humanity. Eventually, in the Hellenistic period, monotheism evolved as the identifying characteristic of the Jewish people, succinctly summarised in the following demand of the Hebrew Bible: 'So acknowledge today and take to heart that the Lord is God in heaven above and on the earth beneath; there is no other' (Deuteronomy 4:39).

Jewish monotheism laid the foundation for the emergence of Christian and Islamic monotheism. We can only briefly touch on this here. Regarding the origins of Christianity as an offshoot of Judaism, the monotheistic idea of a single God was adopted and transformed by the early Christian community, which perceived the historical figure of Jesus of Nazareth as the anticipated

Messiah and thus gradually evolved out of contemporary Judaism. Nevertheless, they continued to worship the Jewish God of Abraham, Isaac, and Jacob, albeit within a modified Trinitarian framework, as delineated in the theological developments of the first centuries. Correspondingly, God's nature must be understood as an indissoluble unity of three persons – God the Father, the Son, and the Holy Spirit – yet, according to Christian understanding, it remains explicitly monotheistic. Monotheistic absolutism and universalism are thereby even reinforced. Following the *Great Commission*, outlined in Matthew 28:19–20, the risen Christ instructs his followers to proclaim the gospel throughout the entire world and to 'make disciples of all nations, baptizing them in the name of the Father and of the Son and of the Holy Spirit, and teaching them to obey everything that I have commanded you'.

Islamic monotheism relies on Adam, Abraham (Ibrāhīm), and Moses (Mūsā) as the first messengers of God within a succession of prophets, culminating in Muhammad, who is revered by Muslims as divinely inspired founder of Islam. Alongside Muhammad, Abraham ranks among the most venerated and extolled figures within Islam, for he is depicted in the Qur'an as 'neither a Jew nor a Christian' (Surah 3:67).[7] As such, he is acknowledged as the first prophet who scorned the erroneous creeds of his time and proclaimed faith in the one and supreme God (Waines 2003: 13–14). Numerous surahs in the Qur'an, believed by Muslims to be the verbatim revelation of God and the principal source of Islamic theology, describe the sublime uniqueness (*tawḥīd*) and sovereignty of Allah – as the most common Arabic title for God has been since pre-Islamic times. As in Judaism and Christianity, the God of the Qur'an is depicted in various ways (Ibrahim 2022: 2–11): as an all-merciful agent who alone is worthy of worship and praise, as an all-powerful creator and sustainer of the universe, transcendent and absolute, without beginning or end, independent and unlimited by spatial or temporal bounds. For instance, Surah 57 states about God:

> Control of the heavens and earth belongs to Him; He gives life and death; He has power over all things. He is the First and the Last; the Outer and the Inner; He has knowledge of all things. [. . .] Believe in God and His Messenger, and give out of what He has made pass down to you: those of you who believe and give will have a great reward.

In summary, the religious finding of a single and supreme God as the creator and ruler of the world gradually laid the foundation for the historical emergence of Judaism, Christianity, and Islam in different epochs. Despite internal differences, God is revered in these religions as the supreme and ultimate deity,

---

[7] Quotations from the Qur'an are taken from The Qur'an. Translated by Muhammad A. S. Abdel Haleem, Oxford 2016.

a benevolent, morally perfect agent who is the creator, guide, and judge of all humankind. In this regard, traditional monotheism includes what I have called previously 'theological absolutism'. To recapitulate: absolutism, as the antithesis of relativism, posits that certain absolute facts, truths, or values exist in specific domains. A fact is absolute if it obtains independently of our theories and conceptual schemes or frameworks. In theological terms, the existence of the unique and supreme God is presumed as an absolute fact. God's being transcends the material universe, is not bound by physical laws and human thought, and does not depend on the cognitive recognition or active worship of believers. In monotheistic theology, the absolute fact of God's existence is closely connected with the notion of 'redemptive universalism', namely his intention to redeem all humanity. God is believed to have created human beings 'in his own image' (Genesis 1:27), so that human mental and moral attributes reflect, in a finite manner, the inconceivable infinity of God's mental and moral attributes.[8] From a theological perspective, this distinct relationship between God and his creatures demonstrates the divine aim of redeeming *all* people from a certain state of deficiency. Consequently, from a theological perspective, the idea of redemptive universalism carries existential significance not only for adherents of monotheism, but also for all humans, regardless of their awareness or belief in it. This detrimental condition is largely interpreted similarly in the three Abrahamic religions, albeit with different accentuations in each case (captivity, sinfulness, egocentrism, or separation from God). To clarify, 'redemptive universalism' solely refers to the divine intention to redeem all humanity, but it does not necessarily imply that God will in fact redeem everyone. Within monotheism, redemption is contingent upon certain conditions on the human side, such as faith, repentance, and obedience.

In general, the transmission of faith is of major importance, with varying emphasis, across all Abrahamic religions, particularly for Christianity and Islam. Nevertheless, evidence for this redemptive universalism can be found in Judaism as well, especially when considering the prophetic vision in Isaiah 2:2–4. This passage anticipates that, at the end of time, many nations will pilgrimage to YHWH and his holy Mount Zion in Jerusalem. There, he will pronounce a universal judgement and bring an end to all wars. Monotheistic absolutism and the experiences of divine guidance have, in various ways, spurred the development of missionary practices to disseminate the faith among non-believers. The universal alignment of monotheism touches upon a key aspect of our topic. Put cautiously, redemptive universalism appears to

---

[8] This is probably the most influential view of the doctrine of the image of God. For other interpretations, see Burdett (2015).

imply that the truth claims of traditional monotheistic belief cannot be solely applied to the religious community of believers alone. In other words, the promise of God's salvation extends beyond the visible religious community of believers, encompassing the possibility of redemption for all of humanity.

Since ancient times, the described religious experience of a supreme deity has led to various theological debates within the monotheistic religions concerning the divine nature and the rational conceivability of God's attributes as depicted in their sacred scriptures. Particularly since medieval theology and philosophy, scholars from Jewish, Christian, and Muslim traditions have engaged in intensive discussions on the various interpretations of classical divine attributes, such as omnipotence, omniscience, and simplicity. The modern question of how faith in the one God should be proclaimed under the current conditions of increasing atheism and scepticism has given rise to various unorthodox theologies, particularly in Christianity. Non-traditional concepts of God are advocated, for instance, in branches of postmodern and postmetaphysical theology (Vanhoozer 2003), in non-standard theism (pantheism, panentheism, process theology, ultimism, fictionalism) (Buckareff & Nagasawa 2016), and within theological anti-realism and non-cognitivism – the view that religious terminology, for instance about the existence of God, has no cognitive meaning (Cupitt 2001). Overall, these dissenting tendencies within or beyond monotheism strive in various ways to dismiss, deconstruct, transform, or abandon fundamental doctrines and ideas of the classical understanding of God. Since these forms of non-orthodox monotheism are arguably not representative of the conception of God in traditional Judaism, Christianity, and Islam, we can set them aside for the purposes of our discussion.

4.2 Revelation and Truth-Objectivism

If there exists a single, supreme, all-powerful, and transcendent divine being who, out of love, willingly created the world and continues to sustain and intervene in it, primarily to draw human beings closer in faith for their salvation, then it is reasonable for these recipients to expect God to provide, as an initial and gratuitous act and beyond what they can discern about him, some form of revelatory evidence about who he is and how to act in response to his offer of redemption. However, the monotheistic focus on divine revelation clearly indicates that an infinite and transcendent God can manifest himself to finite beings only in a *finite* way, and thus must ultimately remain hidden in his essence (Moser 2010: 27–40). Without this elusiveness, faith would not be a free act of profound and fallible trust in God, but rather a predictable reaction, rendering it somehow absurd *not* to believe in the presence of such definite and unequivocal knowledge of his existence.

In monotheistic theology, 'revelation', derived from the Latin *revelatio*, usually signifies the act of removing a covering or concealing 'veil' (in Latin: *velum*) as a divine act of intentional self-disclosure. Each Abrahamic faith uses distinct terms that are cognate to the etymological meaning of the latinate *revelatio*: *hitgalūt* in Hebrew; *apokálypsis* in the Greek of the New Testament; *waḥyu* in Arabic. 'Revelation' can refer either to the process of revealing or to the content that is revealed. The act of revelation, through which God seeks to engage with people directly or indirectly within finite conditions, serves to remove human ignorance and obduracy. It achieves this by both offering an uncoerced relationship of faith with God and providing various forms of evidence regarding God's will. Insofar as God is the creator of all humankind, revelation extends beyond specific nations or people. God is inaccessible apart from revelation; revelation is public but can only be recognised as true through faith and, for many monotheistic traditions, also through reason. The Qur'an summarises this view as follows: 'It is not granted to any mortal that God should speak to him except through revelation or from behind a veil, or by sending a messenger to reveal by His command what He will' (Surah 42:51).

In this respect, theological absolutism in all Abrahamic religions is closely related to the belief in divine revelation, even if its nature and content are interpreted differently by them (Ward 2011: 169–178). Judaism, Christianity, and Islam jointly distinguish between 'general' revelation, in which God manifests himself indirectly in his creation, and 'special' revelation, in which he reveals himself directly to a specific people. In Judaism, the Hebrew Bible recounts numerous instances where God revealed divine messages to prophets, starting with Noah, Abraham, and, most notably, with Moses, who famously encountered God on Mount Sinai. According to Rabbinic tradition, all the teachings of the Torah must be considered as divine revelations given to Moses. The Torah, encompassing the first five books of the Hebrew Bible, is central to Jewish religious life. In Judaism, the Torah's outstanding importance as God's will is undisputed, despite differences in interpretation among various Orthodox and Reform movements. For Christianity, God revealed himself in his relationship with the people of Israel, and fully in Jesus Christ: 'Long ago God spoke to our ancestors in many and various ways by the prophets, but in these last days he has spoken to us by a Son, [...] the exact imprint of God's very being' (Hebrews 1:1–3). The incarnate Christ is considered the ultimate revelation of God, the divine Son of God the Father. Islam, however, rejects this notion of divine incarnation in Jesus. Muslims believe that God revealed the Qur'an to all of humanity as verbatim record of his will through Muhammad, via the angel Gabriel. The Qur'an is believed to be God's flawless final revelation to humanity until Judgement Day.

To comprehend the interdependence between theological absolutism, divine self-disclosure, and truth-objectivism, we must examine the distinction commonly made in this context between 'personal' and 'propositional' revelation (O'Collins 2016: 3–16). In simplified terms, the former means that God shows himself in particular historical events where he seeks to interact with people or individuals and call them to himself. The latter refers to propositions that are asserted or conveyed through his personal revelation (in statements or beliefs) or can be derived from it (from prescriptions, commandments, admonitions, etc.). Especially in Christian theology of the last decades, the concept of personal revelation has received significant endorsement. The rationale behind this view is that the Bible cannot be seen as a series of propositions about a supreme and omnipotent being but, first and foremost, as a multi-layered narrative about how God wants to engage with people, either through particular persons like prophets or Jesus Christ, or by means of individual vocation and guidance. These concerns are certainly justified. However, within recent theological and philosophical discourse on this topic, there is also broad consensus that the two facets of revelation are interconnected. The idea of 'a completely non-cognitive revelation, in which nothing is known either before, or during, or after the revelatory event would be an oxymoron' (O'Collins 2016: 15). A personal divine disclosure without any form of cognitive content that can be directly or indirectly derived from it is hardly conceivable, since, without any accompanying information, the subject of such an apparition would not be clearly identifiable as 'God'. Consequently, 'God could not reveal himself without simultaneously revealing (making knowable) some propositions about himself' (Wahlberg 2020: chap. 1.2). It should be noted that the cognitive content of monotheistic revelations encompasses not only propositions but also non truth-apt knowledge in form of parables, prayers, thanksgivings, or blessings. In summary, a proper understanding of revelation should connect the narrative of personal divine revelation with the cognitive content that is conveyed through it in some form.

Let us focus more closely on propositional revelation. As brief examples, the Bible states that 'the Lord God made the earth and the heavens' (Genesis 2:4), and Jesus claims, 'The Father and I are one' (John 10:30) and 'Whoever has seen me has seen the Father' (John 14:9). The apostle Paul writes: 'For I handed on to you as of first importance what I in turn had received: that Christ died for our sins in accordance with the scriptures, and that he was buried, and that he was raised on the third day in accordance with the scriptures' (1 Corinthians 15: 3–4). Or the Qur'an states about Allah: 'He will cancel the sins of those who believed in Him and acted righteously' (Surah 64:9). Numerous further statements could be cited. These examples indicate that belief in the monotheistic

God entails acknowledging certain metaphysical propositions about him and his will as true: that God is a supreme being; that God created the world; that God desires to forgive sins; and so forth. Particularly striking examples of propositional revelation can be found in the creeds of the Hebrew religions. For instance, the *Shema*, the most venerable prayer and creed in Judaism, states in its first verse, 'Hear, O Israel: YHWH is our God, YHWH is one'. Clearly, it contains the proposition 'There is a single God', which can either be true or false. In Christianity, the *Nicene Creed* begins as follows (in the version of the Latin Church): 'I believe in one God, the Father Almighty, maker of heaven and earth, and of all things visible and invisible.' This belief includes several propositions, such as 'There is an almighty God' and 'God is the maker of heaven and earth'. The *Shahada*, the Islamic creed, reads: 'I bear witness that there is no God but God, and Muhammad is the Messenger of Allah'. Correspondingly, this Islamic belief asserts the propositions 'There is only one God' and 'Muhammad is God's messenger'.

As discussed in Section 2, a proposition is what is asserted by a belief. Propositions are truth-apt in that they can be true or false; for example, either there is a supreme God, or there is not. Due to their propositional content, monotheistic beliefs make metaphysical claims about the truth of God's existence and nature. Nevertheless, they do not refer only to the realm of metaphysics. In Abrahamic monotheism, meta-empirical statements about God are usually tied to empirical facts. For example, Judaism holds that God chose a particular people during a specific historical epoch; Christianity centres on the historical existence of Jesus of Nazareth as the incarnation of the second person of the Trinity; Islam regards the historical figure of Muhammad as divinely inspired prophet. In other words, at the core of monotheistic beliefs, we find both metaphysical and empirical claims about the truth of God's existence and of the various circumstances through which his universal will for redemption has unfolded.

The scriptures present diverse narratives on divine revelation, which, in terms of propositional content, claim to convey *true* messages inspired directly or indirectly by God himself. Numerous examples illustrate this point. The Bible repeatedly points out that the messages about God are 'true'; for instance: 'This is the disciple who is testifying to these things and has written them, and we know that his testimony is true' (John 21:24). The Christian gospel is referred to as the 'word of the truth' (Colossians 1:5). Similarly, the Qur'an states about God's message: 'They ask you [Prophet], 'Is it true?' Say, 'Yes, by my Lord, it is true, and you cannot escape it' (Surah 10:53).

These comments on the significance of truth and revelation in monotheism refer to a pertinent point of our topic. What are the consequences of theological absolutism for the conception of truth claims in monotheism? I argue that monotheistic truth claims about God, which reside at the centre of faith, must be understood as both objective and non-epistemic (or realist), and thus not relative, since they are founded on theological absolutism and redemptive universalism. In short, truth-objectivism should be recognised as a consequence of theological absolutism and redemptive universalism. Consequently, truth relativism in the domain of metaphysical and empirical matters is not compatible with traditional monotheism. This argument will be justified in the last section.

4.3 Anti-Relativism within Monotheism

It has been argued that there are compelling reasons to view monotheism and truth relativism as incompatible. This thesis may not be embraced by all theologians critical of mainstream theism, particularly within the Christian tradition. However, it is unlikely to face serious objections across the broad spectrum of monotheistic theologies in Judaism, Christianity, and Islam. These traditions typically adhere to a more traditional faith orientation aligned with theological absolutism, redemptive universalism, and truth-objectivism, although they may not explicitly use these terms.

Against this backdrop, one might ask whether there has been criticism of relativism within monotheistic theologies, and, if so, which areas have been the focus. It is evident that there can be no anti-relativism without relativism. As indicated in Section 3, serious conceptions of relativism appear to be absent across the broad range of Jewish and Islamic perspectives, and are only present in relation to Christian theology. Neither Jewish nor Islamic theology seems to endorse any distinct approach to monotheistic relativism. In Islam, although there may have been syncretic sects and competing factions with somewhat relativistic inclinations, these tendencies are not characteristic of mainstream Islamic theology (El-Bizri 2020: 20–21). In this regard, scholars of Islamic studies generally agree that 'Islam is not relativist in its spirit' (Shaukat & Basharat 2022: 294) and 'Islam is not relativistic *per se*' (El-Bizri 2020: 21). In contrast, Christianity, particularly within the tradition of the Catholic Church, has maintained a long history of confronting the Western concept of relativism, developing forms of fierce anti-relativism. What might be the reasons for this divergence within monotheistic theologies? Relativistic stances may not have been thoroughly explored and discussed within Jewish and Islamic theologies to date. Alternatively, their reception may not have been as intense as in Western modernity, which has been more strongly influenced by Enlightenment thought and criticism of religion. This modern context still expects Christianity to publicly justify its beliefs to this day.

In the following discussion, we will focus on the long-standing Catholic anti-relativism. Critical views on relativism can also be found in other Christian denominations, although these are less frequent issued as official church statements and more commonly expressed as individual comments on the internet. Since there are recent studies on Catholic anti-relativism (Accetti 2015; Marschler 2020), our focus will be on the criticism made by Joseph Ratzinger, later Pope Benedict XVI. By the term 'Catholic anti-relativism', I refer to the critique that the Magisterium of the Catholic Church has directed towards relativist theories from the end of the nineteenth century to the present day. The Magisterium, entrusted solely to the Pope and to the college of bishops in communion with him, is the Catholic Church's teaching authority for defining and interpreting the word of God in scripture and tradition.

The roots of the magisterial confrontation with relativism can be traced back to the critique of modernism at the end of the nineteenth century. 'Modernism' was the focal point of a campaign within Catholicism against all currents of a new line of thought, often labelled 'modernist' or 'heretical', which sought to reconcile faith with modernity – bridging the gap between the Church's doctrines and dogmas on one hand, and modern philosophy and science on the other. The term 'relativism' was first mentioned in 1884 in a translation of an encyclical by Pope Leo XIII. The first explicit and official use of the term can be found in the address 'Sollemnis conventus' by Pope Pius XII in 1939: 'A certain relativism [. . .] no longer recognises the norm of true and false, good and evil as an immutable moral law. Instead, it seeks to elevate the constantly changing needs of individuals, classes, and states to the highest principle' (my translation). A prominent concern in this early quote resonates throughout almost all declarations of the magisterium, extending to the most recent papal statements by Benedict XVI and Francis: the fear of relativising the truth. For instance, the 1998 encyclical *Fides et Ratio* discusses a 'lack of confidence in truth' in modernity. Modern philosophy is criticised for neglecting the pursuit of truth and thereby paving the way for relativism. Relativist thinking, it is claimed, denies the exclusive nature of truth and assumes 'that all positions are equally valid' (*Fides et Ratio*, art. 5) – anticipating later discussions in philosophical discourse.

The connection between anti-relativism and the defence of objective truth is particularly evident in the theology of Josef Ratzinger. Against the influence of relativism, he considers it a perilous challenge if Christian truth claims are questioned or compromised in any way. Ratzinger once remarked that the relativist doctrine 'has become the central problem for faith in our time' (Ratzinger 2004: 117). In another lecture, he goes even further, stating that 'relativism [. . .] in certain respects has become the real religion of modern men' (Ratzinger 2004: 84). Ratzinger supports the assertion in *Fides et Ratio* that contemporary philosophy is increasingly ignoring the question of objective truth. However, he also extends his critique beyond this observation. Ratzinger perceives relativism as an emerging intellectual attitude that poses the threat of becoming entrenched and dominant in Western culture, society, and thought. In an address, he stated: 'We live at a time that is broadly characterized by a subliminal relativism that penetrates every area of life. Sometimes this relativism becomes aggressive, when it opposes those who say that they know where the truth or meaning of life is to be found' (Ratzinger 2011). This notion of an ingrained relativist attitude in the everyday life of Western societies is further exacerbated in what is arguably Ratzinger's most famous and infamous statement on relativism:

> Today, having a clear faith based on the Creed of the Church is often labelled as fundamentalism. Whereas relativism, that is, letting oneself be 'tossed here and there, carried about by every wind of doctrine', seems the only attitude that can cope with modern times. We are building a dictatorship of relativism that does not recognize anything as definitive and whose ultimate goal consists solely of one's own ego and desires. (Ratzinger 2005)

There is extensive literature on this statement (Perl 2007), ranging from scathing criticism to outright approval. Remarkably, both Runzo and Ratzinger agree on the diagnosis of an emerging 'age of relativism', as Runzo terms it. However, while Runzo welcomes relativism as enriching pluralism and a hallmark of tolerance, Ratzinger foresees the profound danger of a dominant and omnipresent relativist worldview.

How can Ratzinger's stance on anti-relativism be briefly assessed? First, Ratzinger appears justified in firmly emphasising the claim to truth of Christian monotheism. As previously explored, any attempt to relativise theological absolutism, redemptive universalism, and truth-objectivism tends to undermine the very foundations of Christian theology. Second, Ratzinger's characterisation of contemporary society as suffering from a tyranny of relativism seems to be excessive and less convincing. While widespread forms of unreflected 'everyday relativism' may indeed exist, the question remains as to the extent and significance of these attitudes. Numerous political, cultural, social, and religious debates today do not proceed in the 'equal validity' style of a relativistic 'laissez-faire' attitude towards opposing views, but rather as disputes between entrenched and polarised opinions that uncompromisingly claim objective truth. Moreover, Ratzinger's thesis of pervasive relativism lacks reliable empirical evidence. Third, the assertion that the majority of contemporary philosophers have abandoned the question of objective truth is problematic, particularly given the ongoing debates in analytic philosophy and theology on this topic. Fourth, Ratzinger's position appears to lack philosophical nuance because it fails to investigate whether certain forms or versions of relativism might exist that do not necessarily challenge the Christian claim to truth.

5 Monotheism and Relativism

The final section concludes our previous findings and considerations related to our topic 'Monotheism and Relativism'. The central question of this Cambridge Element has been whether, and to what extent, relativist positions are compatible with traditional monotheism. As may have become evident, a general answer to this question seems to be inappropriate, as the term 'relativism' encompasses a wide range of versions, theories, and ideas. In the introduction, I outlined a nuanced perspective on the relationship between relativism and monotheism. The previous analysis has highlighted that different types and versions of relativism should be distinguished concerning their impact on monotheism: truth relativism about metaphysical and empirical matters, moral relativism, truth relativism about questions of taste, and descriptive relativism. This section examines their implications for traditional monotheism. Since the metaphysical assertion that a supreme God exists is pivotal to monotheism, the impact of truth relativism about metaphysical and empirical matters will be the focal point of our analysis.

5.1 Theological Absolutism and Truth Relativism

I argue that relativism concerning metaphysical and empirical matters is not compatible with traditional monotheism, as it would undermine theological absolutism, redemptive universalism, and truth-objectivism. According to monotheistic belief, God has revealed himself as the ultimate reality, the creator of all human beings, and a loving agent whose universal aim is to redeem this world and all its living creatures. To this extent, the revelatory evidence that God has made available pertains to all people and is not confined to those who believe it and follow his expectations. Propositional revelation, as part of the cognitive dimension of God's self-disclosure, should therefore be considered by monotheists to be true objectively and non-epistemically. Consequently, in Abrahamic monotheism – as argued in Section 4.2 – metaphysical truth claims about God are, due to theological absolutism, both objective and non-epistemical (or realist). Truth-objectivism should be understood as an implication of theological absolutism and redemptive universalism. This argument can be succinctly explained as follows:

(1) God has manifested himself – as the supreme, transcendent, and morally perfect being – and thereby conveyed revelatory evidence of his absolute existence and universal redemptive aim to all people.

(2) Historically, this revelatory evidence has underpinned the emergence of monotheism and, epistemologically, has justified beliefs in God's absolute existence and his universal redemptive aim.

(3) From the perspective of monotheism, these beliefs about God are not true relatively but objectively.

(4) From the perspective of (normative) alethic relativism in the domain of metaphysics, these beliefs about God are not true objectively but relatively.

(5) Therefore, monotheism and alethic relativism in the domain of metaphysics are not compatible.

To summarise, if a supreme God exists as an absolute fact, independent of the material universe and human thought (theological absolutism), and if God has created all human beings and seeks to redeem them through a faith-based relationship (redemptive universalism), then monotheistic beliefs about God – derived theologically from divine revelation and partly summarised in creeds – should be considered true objectively and non-epistemically (truth-objectivism). The two properties of truth are closely intertwined. 'True objectively' means that a claim is true independently of our epistemic status and our ability to confirm or conceive of it. 'True non-epistemically' indicates that a claim is true if what it asserts actually is the case, irrespective of whether and to what extent we can justify or verify it. In contrast, 'true relatively' signifies, within the context of alethic relativism in the field of metaphysics, that claims about God are necessarily true only in a relative sense, dependent on the specific monotheistic framework or belief system. Consequently, such claims do not apply to other religious or non-religious frameworks or belief systems. The contrast between objective and relative concepts of truth became evident when we analysed the two approaches to monotheistic relativism in Section 3. Among other critical points, Runzo's '*Dependency principle of religious relativism*' and Smith's repudiation of realism are in conflict with truth-objectivism.

Overall, alethic relativism challenges both theological absolutism and redemptive universalism, thereby calling into question the objectivity of monotheistic truth claims. This conclusion should also be considered in light of the four features of normative relativism discussed in Section 2.

1. The first feature of relativism, 'dependency', posits that beliefs are not objectively true but relatively, dependent on a specific framework, perspective, or context. As previously outlined, classical monotheism subscribes to an objective and realist conception of truth. The truth of propositional revelation is not contingent upon a particular monotheistic framework or an individual's epistemic ability to justify it. For monotheism, the claim that there is a supreme and transcendent God is true if such a God indeed exists, independent of our

belief in its truth or our epistemic faculties to verify it. In other words, the absolute fact of God's existence serves as the truth-maker for monotheistic truth claims, and not the religious framework in which it is believed. If there really exists a supreme and transcendent God, this claim holds true universally, not just within the framework of monotheism. It would remain true even if, hypothetically, there were no more monotheists left in the world to believe it.

Importantly, the defence of alethic realism does not exempt monotheistic theologians from the responsibility to provide reasons and arguments for the existence of God – and the same applies to atheists, who deny it. However, the epistemic capacities to justify either the existence or non-existence of this supreme being do not determine the ontological matter of its existence. In discussing metaphysical and empirical matters, conditions of justification should not be conflated with conditions of truth. In this regard, it becomes evident that epistemic or anti-realist relativism carries serious and far-reaching consequences for the idea of traditional monotheism. Without the conception of objective principles or facts, knowledge derived from divine revelation – upon which religious teachings are build – could no longer claim to be absolutely true, irrespective of whether we deem ourselves epistemically justified in holding it to be true. Thus, an epistemic or anti-realist conception of truth poses a problem for the monotheistic idea of God. William P. Alston has stated that 'a nonrealist interpretation radically deviates from the traditional Christian understanding of its faith' (Alston 1995: 57). This assessment also applies to its relationships with Judaism and Islam.

To substantiate the correlation between monotheism and truth-objectivism, it may be useful to consider the opposite scenario and interpret the monotheistic conception of God from a relativist perspective. If we were to question whether God exists independently of our awareness of him, and if his existence depended solely on somehow justified beliefs of a specific monotheistic community, the concept of a transcendent God might transform into a human construct, myth, or symbol. This notion of the divine could certainly serve as a source of orientation for a group or an individual; however, God's objective existence in the world and his universal redemptive appeal to all people would no longer play a decisive role. Under the influence of truth relativism, the focus of monotheistic theology might exclusively shift to epistemic concerns, such as the plurality of specific concepts of the divine, while neglecting the pivotal ontological question of whether the divine referent of faith truly exists, independent of believers' notions and perceptions. From this relativist perspective, there could be as many divine referents as there are versions and assumptions of faith. As a consequence, monotheism, traditionally focussed on the existence of a single supreme God, might gradually transition to a polytheistic framework characterised by a variety of distinct divine beings or symbols.

2. The second feature of normative relativism, 'conflict resolution', posits that disagreements between conflicting or irreconcilable positions can be resolved by relativising beliefs to specific frameworks. 'Relativism is a way to resolve disagreement,' as we quoted Steven D. Hales. Joseph Runzo has favoured his religious relativism as a theory for mediating and resolving conflicts between different world religions. Given recent studies on the relationship between monotheism and religious diversity (Baghramian 2012; Trigg 2020), we can focus solely on the impact of relativism. First, it is questionable whether alethic relativism possesses the necessary resources to manage and resolve interreligious disagreement. One might even argue that in interreligious truth relativism, conflicts and disagreements between religions are unlikely to arise due to the relativisation of truth claims. Thus, how should we assess the relationship between relativism and interreligious conflicts? Clearly, although conflicts can indeed be destructive and express intolerance, they are not necessarily so. Often, conflicts prove to be conducive to problem-solving in the long term, even when waged under challenging circumstances. Conflicts might be essential for progress in interreligious understanding, when accompanied by attitudes such as rationality, tolerance, empathy, and a willingness to learn (McKim 2019: 48–58). Without external criticism, disagreement, and sometimes conflict about truth, religions may risk degenerating into intractable dogmatism or even idolatry.

Second, it is doubtful whether the majority of religious adherents would embrace truth relativism as a normative theory for understanding their own faith and resolving interreligious conflicts. If the claim to objectivity is abandoned, the transition from monotheistic absolutism to truth relativism would completely change the belief system and theological framework of their religion (Trigg 1983: 299). For instance, without a commitment to truth-objectivism, theologians might no longer find it necessary to critically engage with other religious and non-religious positions, such as atheism. In other words, to 'accept religious relativism as a solution to the problem of diversity is to deprive religion of its power to convince or persuade the nonbeliever' (Baghramian 2012: 307). To this extent, the advantages of alethic relativism as a conflict resolver remain unclear. Instead of settling conflicts, it appears to silence or avoid disagreement by relativising truth claims. This negative conclusion, however, does not apply to descriptive relativism (as further examined in Section 5.4).

3. The third feature of relativism, 'non-absolutism', asserts that no absolute viewpoint exists for adjudicating a belief or framework as true in an absolute or objective manner. According to 'theological absolutism', God represents an absolute reality in monotheism. While human beings cannot adopt a 'God's eye

view' due to their finite perspectives, monotheists attribute this absolute viewpoint solely to God himself. Strikingly, both relativists and absolutists trace back the idea of absolutism to the monotheistic belief in a transcendent God (Bloor 2020: 395; Trigg 2020: 51; Rorty 2021: xxvii–xxxiii, 1). For instance, David Bloor argues that it was primarily the Christian belief in the absolute truth of God that stimulated the concept of absolute truth in philosophy, and later, as a corollary, relativism as its counterpart. 'The current debate over relativism is a re-run of the traditional debate over the truth of religion. Relativists are the unbelievers; anti-relativists are the believers. The belief in absolute truth is a belief in God, and anti-relativism is a belief in God in disguise' (Bloor 2020: 395). Even if this assessment may seem overly contrastive, it clearly demonstrates that the feature 'non-absolutism' is at odds with traditional monotheism.

4. According to the fourth feature of normative relativism, 'equal validity', all beliefs within a given domain are equally valid because they are all true relatively, in conjunction with 'dependency' and 'non-absolutism'. The previous discussion has sought to demonstrate that this feature of relativism is inconsistent with the self-understanding of monotheism. Religious truth-objectivism involves some form of exclusivism. In various forms, monotheistic exclusivism posits that one's own religious tradition is largely true regarding the existence and nature of God, while other religions that contradict these beliefs are considered false and 'excluded' from the truth or salvation offered by the home religion. In theistic theologies and philosophies, various suggestions have been proposed to reconcile exclusivism with redemptive universalism (for Christianity, see Moser 2010: 232–254). It is common understanding that the diversity of world religions provides varied and contradictory responses to the question of whether there is a single and supreme God. From the perspective of monotheism, a polytheistic religion that denies the existence of such a God would not be regarded as 'equally valid' compared to a monotheistic religion. According to the law of non-contradiction, mutually exclusive beliefs cannot both be 'equally' true – and if they are not equally true, they cannot be equally valid. The idea that all religions or religious beliefs are somehow 'equally valid' as they are all relatively true, is in conflict with traditional monotheism and truth-objectivism.

To further illustrate this incompatibility, let us briefly revisit the discussion of relativist approaches by Hales and Rovane in Section 2. As quoted, Hales presented his idea of relativism as a 'solution to disagreement', provided that there is both irresolvable disagreement and no alternative solutions for resolving it are available. In contrast, an adherent of monotheism may contest that relativism offers a 'solution' to the irresolvable disagreement with a polytheist. First, as previously indicated, relativism seems to explain away rather than resolve this dispute through the strategy of relativisation. Second, contrary to

Hales's suggestion, a rational alternative solution may be readily available: maintain and justify one's own position until there are reasons not to; tolerate the other view without coercion or reprobation, and perhaps even learn from it. In this respect, Rovane's relativist conception of 'multimundialism' has taken the idea of an ontological plurality of insulated and 'equally valid' worlds much more seriously. As quoted, according to Rovane 'we shall have to acknowledge [. . .] that we have nothing to teach, and nothing to learn from, other people who reside outside of those boundaries – that is the practical implication of their inhabiting a different world'. However, this relativistic scenario is completely different from and incompatible with the picture monotheism draws of the world, as we discussed in the last section and need not repeat here.

5.2 Objective Morality and Moral Relativism

Based on the findings from the previous section, we will briefly outline a major impact of moral relativism on monotheism. Within the field of the Abrahamic religions, a variety of different and often incompatible ideas of morality exists. For example, a liberal Jewish view may hold that some ethical commandments and ritual rules are universal and objective, while others must be adapted to current conditions. In Christianity, with its various denominations, there is no universally agreed-upon consensus on the exact meaning of Christian morality, the form of objectivity or normativity that should be attached to specific ethical commandments, rules, and values, or even if there exists at all 'a unique moral code of such and such a type' (Harman 2001: 171). The Bible reveals a plurality of ethical perspectives and viewpoints (Verhey 2012: 42–45), leading to diverse moral traditions and ethical approaches within Christianity, such as deontological, teleological, virtue, liberation, natural law ethics. This diversity has prompted varied judgements on specific moral issues, including debates on homosexuality or abortion (Lovin 2012). In Islamic ethics, the Qur'an serves as the primary scriptural source for moral teachings. Despite a widespread adherence to theological absolutism in both Sunni and Shia Islam, different theological schools have emerged, stemming from disparate interpretations of divine doctrine, jurisprudence, and ethics. For instance, *Ash'arism*, a major Sunni school, largely denies the universality of moral truths, insisting that an action is morally good only if commanded by God. In contrast, *Maturidism*, another orthodox Sunni school, supports the notion of a universal objective morality that can be recognised by reason.

Theologically, this diversity should be viewed as an expression of the historical development of religious culture. A central tenet across all monotheistic traditions is the belief that God himself established a binding moral order through creation. In this regard, religious ethics are derived from the sacred scriptures, which understand God as the ultimate source of moral guidance (Moser 2022). God is believed to be a morally perfect being who alone is worthy of worship. By regarding God as the originator of all moral goodness, Judaism, Christianity, and Islam traditionally adhere to moral realism and assert the existence of objective morality, the idea that moral facts or values exist independently of our epistemic approach to them. In simplified terms, moral realism holds that ethical propositions are true if they correspond to an objective moral fact. The significance of moral realism for monotheism is evident from the theological link between divine creation and moral order. Monotheistic belief holds that God created not only the material world but also an inherent moral order, to which humans are expected to adhere. In this respect, the concept of objective morality, which stems from God's plan of creation, is crucial for monotheism. Examples of such divinely ordained objective morality include the *Mitzvot* in Judaism, the 613 divine commandments that Jews are to follow, the Christian concept of *lex naturalis* or natural law, a system of divine norms intrinsic to the natural order or human reason, and the *Sharia*, the Islamic law revealed by God.

Insofar as metaethical and normative versions of moral relativism deny the existence of objective morality, they stand in opposition to the conception of divine law. In summary, not only does alethic relativism concerning metaphysical matters conflict with traditional monotheism, but moral relativism also appears to be at odds with it, at least with the vast majority of its traditions.

5.3 Theistic Belief and Matters of Taste

In Section 2, we briefly examined core ideas of 'New Relativism', a version of local alethic relativism that applies to matters of subjective taste and predilections. Notably, this version and the debate surrounding it are not merely a niche discussion within the broader debates on relativism; rather, they have been at the forefront of interest in recent years. How does this version of alethic relativism relate to the monotheistic conception of truth?

Thus far, the analysis in this section has been confined to the significance of metaphysical and moral truth claims about God, which are central to Abrahamic monotheism. Religions are complex cultural systems encompassing a variety of beliefs, practices, rituals, ethics, and more. Focussing on beliefs, there is a wide spectrum ranging from central beliefs that shape the respective religious identity, to peripheral or minor beliefs that might have been added over the course of history and are less essential for the religion. Should all claims of Abrahamic monotheism be regarded as objectively true? The answer is no, particularly in the religiously less significant domain of matters of taste. For example, the Book of Psalms states about the king or Messiah, the future saviour of the Jews: 'I address my verses to the king [. . .]. You are the most handsome of men; grace is poured upon your lips; therefore God has blessed you for ever' (Psalm 45: 1–2). From a Christian perspective, there could be a disagreement about the claim 'Frankincense from South Arabia is better suited for the liturgical worship of God's altar than that from India.' The proper and measured recitation of the Qur'an (*tajwīd*) is of great importance in Islam. Since there are different views in the Islamic world about which *qāri'* (reciter) has performed best, Muslim A might claim 'Abdul Basit is the best *qāri'* of the Qur'an to date', while Muslim B might disagree and reply, 'No, Mishary bin Rashid Alafasy did it best'.

These examples illustrate 'disputes of inclination' relating to controversial questions of religious taste and preference (although the Jewish example may not be interpreted literally). In the framework of 'New Relativism', a relativist might argue that regarding the Islamic example, the same proposition, 'Abdul Basit is the best *qāri'* of the Qur'an to date', is true for Muslim A relative to her context of assessment and false for Muslim B relative to his context of assessment. Even though A and B genuinely disagree, both positions could be without epistemic fault and thus equally true or valid in a relative sense. In the context of disagreement on matters of taste, there appear to be no objective facts available to serve as truth-makers for propositions – unlike questions of whether a supreme God exists or whether the prophet Muhammad really lived. Against 'New Relativism', one might argue, first, that it fails to represent genuine disagreement; second, that proper training in expertise on matters of preference could function as a possible arbiter in these cases; or, third, that detaching the notion of truth *simpliciter* (or objective truth) comes at a high cost to our ordinary understanding of truth (Cappelen & Hawthorne 2009: 134). We do not need to take a stand here on whether 'New Relativism' is convincing (for a critique, see Baghramian & Coliva 2020: 68–84). It suffices to acknowledge that the 'new' relativists present some compelling arguments and *could* be correct about matters of taste.

What are the implications of this version of relativism for our topic? Although some cases of disagreement on matters of subjective taste may be religiously relevant in certain respects, our analysis has clarified that theistic truth claims about these matters do not hold the same significance as theistic truth claims about metaphysical, epistemological, moral, or historical issues. The monotheistic affirmation that a supreme God exists is not presented as a remark about a believer's taste (Moser 2010: 20). Ultimately, a fundamental difference remains between disagreements on metaphysical matters ('Is there a supreme divine being?') and disagreements on matters of subjective preference ('Which frankincense is best for certain religious purposes?'). From the perspective of traditional monotheism, only disagreements on metaphysical, empirical, and, to some extent, moral matters necessitate an objective and non-epistemic understanding of truth for resolution. Hence, relativist approaches to the realm of subjective taste and predilections are unlikely to pose significant challenges for absolutists about such matters.

Consequently, it seems possible to be both a monotheistic absolutist and an aesthetic relativist simultaneously. In other words, one could be a truth absolutist on metaphysical matters, such as the existence of God, and a truth relativist on aesthetic issues. Given that such a combination is conceivable even from a monotheist's perspective, a nuanced position should be adopted regarding our general question of whether monotheism is compatible with relativism.

5.4 Religious Plurality and Descriptive Relativism

In Section 2.1.1, we have analysed the distinction between descriptive and normative relativism. While the former aims to describe the relativity of beliefs stemming from different cultural, social, or religious contexts, the latter prescribes a norm according to which beliefs are always relative to particular frameworks. We have also offered some arguments as to why descriptive relativism should be relevant not only for anthropologists or field study researchers. Let us revisit the example of descriptive relativism mentioned previously: 'The concept of a single transcendent God is relative to specific monotheistic religions'. Although all three Abrahamic monotheistic religions share the common practice of worshipping a single transcendent God, their specific concepts of this deity differ considerably and partly even appear to be incompatible with each other. This is evident, for instance, in the contrasting ideas of *tawḥīd*, which emphasises the oneness of God in Islam, and the Christian concept of the Trinity. Since monotheists must acknowledge the empirical fact that the concept of a single supreme God is relative to each monotheistic religion, they may, or should, also endorse descriptive relativism. Consequently, this weak type of relativism should not pose a challenge to monotheism. On the contrary, descriptive relativism may even be conducive to monotheism for two reasons. First, it highlights the empirical contingency in the adoption of religious beliefs, suggesting that these beliefs can vary based on different contexts. Second, in the context of diverse religious beliefs and practices, it may promote epistemic modesty in asserting theological absolutism, thereby encouraging a more humble and reflective approach to claims of objective truth.

1. The increased awareness of global religious diversity may be one reason for acknowledging the insights of descriptive relativism. Accordingly, religious beliefs are profoundly dependent on and relative to certain cognitive frameworks in terms of their origin and emergence, but not in terms of their validity or truth. This important distinction about the relativity of beliefs should be kept in mind. Since the descriptive relativist's position is not normative, it does not preclude general assumptions, such as the idea that most religions share a common and unifying longing for a spiritual meaning of life. At first glance, the diagnosis that religious beliefs are largely influenced and shaped by cultural and cognitive frameworks may seem obvious. However, many religious adherents apparently do not accept this premise, as they despise other religions and often seem unwilling or unable to recognise that followers of these religions usually have valid reasons for adopting their faith. We previously quoted Runzo's statement that belonging to a religious community and adhering to specific doctrines is rarely a matter of rational and balanced consideration, but largely 'an accident of birth'. There are two facets to this perspective.

Empirically, it indeed seems likely, for instance, that a Western monotheist would hold different religious beliefs if she were born into a predominantly polytheistic culture. While this hypothesis reveals nothing about the truth of monotheism or polytheism, it does elucidate the impact of diverse, entrenched worldviews and our habitual adherence to them in daily life. Yet, the relativity of beliefs concerning their origin and their truth should be considered as two distinct matters. As for the latter, believers can and should learn about other religions, and they may, at some point, decide to convert to another belief system if they find that their inherited faith is no longer convincing or simply wrong. Even though this freedom is not always politically granted, numerous examples demonstrate that conversion is possible. In this respect, descriptive relativism may foster the acceptance and recognition of religious plurality among monotheists, especially those inclined towards religious fundamentalism, which typically disregards and often even actively opposes other faith traditions. Since this recognition does not preclude the ongoing interreligious quest for truth, it is possible to be both a descriptive relativist and a religious absolutist at the same time.

2. In addition, descriptive relativism may sensitise adherents of monotheism not only to the emergence of religious diversity and the various reasons for adopting beliefs but also to practising their faith with epistemic modesty in the face of religious plurality. In public discussions, interfaith conflicts, intolerance, and violence are very often attributed to religious absolutism, which is deemed to be closely intertwined with fundamentalism. For some scholars, monotheism has left behind a particularly 'violent legacy' because, as the argument goes, it

has contributed to the emergence of fundamentalism, exclusivism, and religious intolerance (Schwartz 1997; Sloterdijk 2009). Notably, the Egyptologist Jan Assmann has argued that the Hebrew Bible introduced the concept of 'absolute truth', linked to the oneness of God, as a new monotheistic idea into Western intellectual history (Assmann 2009: 13). In his view, the revolutionary notion of God's absolute truth has laid the historical foundation for the intolerant and violent exclusion of other religions and worldviews incompatible with monotheistic absolutism (Assmann 2009: 15–23).

Echoing these criticisms from a relativist perspective, David Bloor contends that the 'truly dangerous people abroad in the world today are all absolutists'. In his view, it is 'the dictatorship of absolutism, and the war of absolute against absolute' that should be feared (Bloor 2007: 279). Allegations like these are certainly overstated and misrepresentative. Space does not permit a further discussion here. However, as previously emphasised, even if monotheistic belief asserts objective truth, it could still be erroneous. Faith should be understood as a profound and unwavering trust in God, albeit inherently fallible. Inasmuch as the belief system of monotheistic truth-objectivism explicitly refrains from assuming a 'God's eye view', it remains, epistemologically, one perspective among many in the world. Consequently, adopting descriptive relativism should not lead to doubting the truth of monotheistic beliefs, but rather to fostering an awareness of their potential shortcomings in terms of intolerance, self-righteousness, or a reluctance to learn about other religions.

Monotheistic exclusivism encompasses various interpretations, including inclusivist construals, which may recognise the salvific force of other religions or acknowledge the inclusivity of truth within their doctrines (Moser 2011: 85–87). As noted in Section 4.1, Abrahamic monotheism exhibits an inclusivist, universal alignment, recognising God as a loving and redeeming deity for all human beings. Descriptive relativism, which captures the plurality of religious beliefs, may support monotheists in adopting a more inclusive and modest path of faith, while also rejecting fundamentalist or fanatical types of exclusivism.

5.5 Conclusion

The central question of this Element has revolved around whether, and to what extent, relativism is compatible with traditional monotheism. Drawing from our previous analysis, we can now offer a brief conclusion. First, truth relativism concerning metaphysical and empirical matters is not compatible with monotheism. The monotheistic principles of theological absolutism, redemptive universalism, and truth-objectivism contradict the normative relativist notion that the truth of beliefs is invariably dependent on specific viewpoints, thus leaving no non-relative stance from which to adjudicate the objective truth of competing claims. Second, moral relativism should also be considered as opposed to the central tenets of traditional monotheism. Metaethical and normative versions of moral relativism conflict with the concept of objective morality promoted by the idea of divine law. Third, truth relativism concerning questions of subjective taste has no important impact on monotheism. Conflicts over matters of taste and predilections do not hold particular significance for monotheistic belief. Yet, disagreements on metaphysical matters must be clearly distinguished from disagreements on matters of aesthetic preference. According to traditional monotheism, only the former type of disagreement necessitates a realist understanding of truth for resolution. Fourth, descriptive relativism may offer instructive insights for theistic belief, as it has the potential to sensitise monotheists to the empirical foundations of adopting religious beliefs. Furthermore, it may encourage a modest, tolerant, and non-fundamentalist proclamation of one's faith in relation to competing religious views.

Therefore, the question of whether monotheism and relativism are compatible requires a nuanced response.

References

Accetti, C. I. (2015). *Relativism and Religion: Why Democratic Societies Do Not Need Moral Absolutes*. New York: Columbia University Press.

Alston, W. P. (1995). Realism and the Christian Faith. *International Journal for Philosophy of Religion*, 38(1–3), 37–60.

Alston, W. P. (1996). *A Realist Conception of Truth*. Ithaca: Cornell University Press.

Assmann, J. (2009). *The Price of Monotheism*. Translated by R. Savage. Stanford: Stanford University Press.

Baghramian, M. (2004). *Relativism*. New York: Routledge.

Baghramian, M. (2012). Relativism and Religious Diversity. In F. O'Rourke, ed., *Human Destinies: Philosophical Essays in Memory of Gerald Hanratty*. Notre Dame, IN: University of Notre Dame Press, 290–311.

Baghramian, M., ed. (2014). *The Many Faces of Relativism*. New York: Routledge.

Baghramian, M. & Carter, A. J. (2020). Relativism. In *The Stanford Encyclopedia of Philosophy*, https://plato.stanford.edu/entries/relativism.

Baghramian, M. & Coliva, A. (2020). *Relativism*. London & New York: Routledge.

Beddor, B. (2020). Relativism and Expressivism. In M. Kusch, ed., *The Routledge Handbook of Philosophy of Relativism*. New York: Routledge, 528–539.

Berger, P. L., ed. (2010). *Between Relativism and Fundamentalism: Religious Resources for a Middle Position*. Grand Rapids: William B. Eerdmans.

Bilgrami, A. (2010). Realism and Relativism. In M. Krausz, ed., *Relativism. A Contemporary Anthology*. New York: Columbia University Press, 194–221.

Bloom, A. (1987). *The Closing of the American Mind: How Higher Education Has Failed Democracy and Impoverished the Souls of Today's Students*. New York: Simon and Schuster.

Bloor, D. (2007). Epistemic Grace: Antirelativism as Theology in Disguise. In J. M. Perl, ed., *A Dictatorship of Relativism? Symposium in Response to Cardinal Ratzinger's Last Homily*. Common Knowledge, 13 (2–3). Durham, NC: Duke University Press, 250–280.

Bloor, D. (2011). Relativism and the Sociology of Scientific Knowledge. In S. D. Hales, ed., *A Companion to Relativism*. Oxford: Wiley-Blackwell, 433–455.

Bloor, D. (2020). Antinomianism. In M. Kusch, ed., *The Routledge Handbook of Philosophy of Relativism*. London & New York: Routledge, 388–397.

Boghossian, P. (2006). *Fear of Knowledge: Against Relativism and Constructivism.* Oxford: Oxford University Press.

Boncompagni, A. (2020). Relativism and Pragmatism. In M. Kusch, ed., *The Routledge Handbook of Philosophy of Relativism.* New York: Routledge, 124–132.

Brown, M. (2008). Cultural Relativism 2.0. *Current Anthropology,* 49, 363–383.

Buckareff, A. & Nagasawa, Y. (2016). *Alternative Concepts of God: Essays on the Metaphysics of the Divine.* Oxford: Oxford University Press.

Burdett, M. S. (2015). The Image of God and Human Uniqueness: Challenges from the Biological and Information Sciences. *Expository Times,* 127, 3–10.

Cappelen, H. & Hawthorne, J. (2009). *Relativism and Monadic Truth.* Oxford: Oxford University Press.

Carter, J. A. (2016). Epistemology and Relativism. In *The Internet Encyclopedia of Philosophy,* https://iep.utm.edu/epis-rel.

Corradetti, C. (2022). *Relativism and Human Rights: A Theory of Pluralist Universalism.* 2nd ed. Dordrecht: Springer.

Cupitt, D. (2001). *Reforming Christianity.* Santa Rosa, CA: Polebridge Press.

Echeverria, E. (2014). Relativism – Ancilla Theologiae et Fidei? Not so Fast! *Calvin Theological Journal,* 49, 258–282.

El-Bizri, N. (2020). Relativism in the Islamic traditions. In M. Kusch, ed., *The Routledge Handbook of Philosophy of Relativism.* New York: Routledge, 20–28.

Flood, G. D. (2020). *Hindu Monotheism.* Cambridge: Cambridge University Press.

Fish, S. (2001). Condemnation Without Absolutes. *New York Times,* 15 October 2001, www.nytimes.com/2001/10/15/opinion/condemnation-without-absolutes.html.

García-Carpintero, M. & Kölbel, M., eds. (2008). *Relative Truth.* Oxford: Oxford University Press.

Gottwald, S. (2015). Many-Valued Logic. In *The Stanford Encyclopedia of Philosophy,* https://plato.stanford.edu/entries/logic-manyvalued.

Haack, S. (1998). *Manifesto of a Passionate Moderate. Unfashionable Essays.* Chicago: University of Chicago Press.

Hales, S. D., ed. (2011). *A Companion to Relativism.* Oxford: Wiley-Blackwell.

Hales, S. D. (2014). Motivations for Relativism as a Solution to Disagreements. *Philosophy,* 89(1), 63–82.

Hales, S. D. (2020). Self-refutation. In M. Kusch, ed., *The Routledge Handbook of Philosophy of Relativism.* New York: Routledge, 283–291.

Harman, G. (2001). Is There a Single True Morality? In P. K. Moser & T. L. Carson, eds., *Moral Relativism: A Reader.* Oxford: Oxford University Press, 165–184.

Hick, J. (2004). *An Interpretation of Religion: Human Responses to the Transcendent*. 2nd ed. New York: Palgrave Macmillan.

Ibrahim, C. (2022). *Islam and Monotheism*. Cambridge: Cambridge University Press.

Irlenborn, B. (2016). *Relativismus*. Berlin & New York: De Gruyter.

Irlenborn, B. & Seewald, M., eds. (2020). *Relativismus und christlicher Wahrheitsanspruch: Philosophische und theologische Perspektiven*. Freiburg: Verlag Karl Alber.

Kölbel, M. (2002). *Truth Without Objectivity*. London & New York: Routledge.

Kölbel, M. (2011). Global Relativism and Self-Refutation. In S. D. Hales, ed., *A Companion to Relativism*. Oxford: Wiley-Blackwell, 11–30.

Kusch, M. (2019). Relativist Stances, Virtues And Vices. *Aristotelian Society Supplementary Volume*, 93(1), 271–291.

Kusch, M., ed. (2020a). *The Routledge Handbook of Philosophy of Relativism*. New York: Routledge.

Kusch, M. (2020b). *Relativism in the Philosophy of Science*. Cambridge: Cambridge University Press.

Lovin, R.-W. (2012). Moral traditions in eastern and western Christianity. In R. Gill, ed., *The Cambridge Companion to Christian Ethics*. 2nd ed. Cambridge: Cambridge University Press, 16–27.

Lynch, M.-P. (2011). Truth Relativism and Truth Pluralism. In S. D. Hales, ed., *A Companion to Relativism*. Oxford: Wiley-Blackwell, 85–101.

MacFarlane, J. (2008). Boghossian, Bellarmine, and Bayes. *Philosophical Studies*, 141(3), 391–398.

MacFarlane, J. (2022). Equal Validity and Disagreement: Comments on Baghramian and Coliva's *Relativism*. *Analysis*, 82(3), 499–506.

MacIntyre, A. (1985). Relativism, Power and Philosophy. *Proceedings and Addresses of the American Philosophical Association*, 59(1), 5–22.

Margolis, J. (2010). The Truth about Relativism. In M. Krausz, ed., *Relativism. A Contemporary Anthology*. New York: Columbia University Press, 100–123.

Marschler, T. (2020). Anspruch auf Wahrheit: Das kirchliche Lehramt über 'Relativismus'. In B. Irlenborn & M. Seewald, eds., *Relativismus und christlicher Wahrheitsanspruch. Philosophische und theologische Perspektiven*. Freiburg: Verlag Karl Alber, 158–192.

McKim, R. (2019). *Religious Diversity and Religious Progress*. Cambridge: Cambridge University Press.

Meister, C. (2006). *Building Belief. Constructing Faith from the Ground Up*. Eugene, OR: Wipf & Stock.

Meister, C., ed. (2011). *The Oxford Handbook of Religious Diversity*. Oxford: Oxford University Press.

Miller, A. (2021). Realism. In *The Stanford Encyclopedia of Philosophy*, https://plato.stanford.edu/archives/win2021/entries/realism.

Misak, C. (2013). *The American Pragmatists*. Oxford: Oxford University Press.

Moser, P. K. (2010). *The Evidence for God. Religious Knowledge Reexamined*. Cambridge: Cambridge University Press.

Moser, P. K. (2011). Religious Exclusivism. In C. Meister, ed., *The Oxford Handbook of Religious Diversity*. Oxford: Oxford University Press, 77–88.

Moser, P. K. (2022). *Divine Guidance: Moral Attraction in Action*. Cambridge: Cambridge University Press.

Moser, P. K. & Carson, T. L., eds. (2001). *Moral Relativism: A Reader*. Oxford: Oxford University Press.

Norris, C. (2011). Anti-Realism and Relativism. In S. D. Hales, ed., *A Companion to Relativism*. Oxford: Oxford University Press, 489–508.

O'Collins, G. (2016). *Revelation. Towards a Christian Interpretation of God's Self-Revelation in Jesus Christ*. Oxford: Oxford University Press.

O'Grady, P. (2002). *Relativism*. London & New York: Routledge.

Park, S. (2011). Defence of Cultural Relativism. *Cultura: International Journal of Philosophy of Culture and Axiology*, 8 (1), 159–170.

Perl, J. M., ed. (2007). *A Dictatorship of Relativism? Symposium in Response to Cardinal Ratzinger's Last Homily*. Common Knowledge, 13(2–3): Durham, NC: Duke University Press.

Plato (1988). *Theaetetus. Sophist*. Translated by H. N. Fowler. Cambridge, MA: Harvard University Press.

Popper, K. (2020). *The Open Society and Its Enemies*. One-Volume Edition. Foreword by G. Soros, Princeton, NJ: Princeton University Press.

Ratzinger, J. (2004). *Truth and Tolerance. Christian Belief and World Religions*. San Francisco: Ignatius Press.

Ratzinger, J. (2005). *Homily 'Pro Eligendo Romano Pontifice'*. Addressed to the College of Cardinals in the Vatican Basilica (18 April 2005), www.vatican.va/gpII/documents/homily-pro-eligendo-pontifice.

Ratzinger, J. [Pope Benedict XVI] (2011). *Address of His Holiness to the Catholic Lay Faithful*. Apostolic Journey of His Holiness Pope Benedict XVI to Germany (24 September 2011), www.vatican.va/content/benedict-xvi/en/speeches/2011.

Römer, T. (2015). The Invention of God. Translated by R. Geuss. Cambridge, MA: Harvard University Press.

Rorty, R. (1979). *Philosophy and the Mirror of Nature*. Princeton: Princeton University Press.

Rorty, R. (2021). *Pragmatism as Anti-Authoritarianism*. Edited by E. Mendieta. Cambridge, MA: Harvard University Press.

Rovane, C. (2013). *The Metaphysics and Ethics of Relativism*. Cambridge, MA: Harvard University Press.

Runzo, J. (1986). *Reason, Relativism and God*. London: Macmillan.

Runzo, J. (2008). Religious Relativism. In C. Meister, ed., *The Philosophy of Religion Reader*. New York: Routledge, 60–78 [first published under the title: God, Commitment, and Other Faiths: Pluralism vs. Relativism. *Faith and Philosophy*, 5(1988), 343–364].

Runzo, J. (2011). Pluralism and Relativism. In C. Meister, ed., *The Oxford Handbook of Religious Diversity*. Oxford: Oxford University Press, 61–76.

Sankey, H. (2022). Objective Facts. *Metaphysica: International Journal for Ontology and Metaphysics*, 23(1), 117–121.

Schwartz, R. (1997). *The Curse of Cain: The Violent Legacy of Monotheism*. Chicago: University of Chicago Press.

Shaukat, M. A. & Basharat, T. (2022). A Study of Relativistic Theory of Ethics in the Light of Islamic Theory of Morality. *Journal of Islamic Thought and Civilization*, 12(2), 286–298.

Sloterdijk, P. (2009). *God's Zeal. The Battle of the Three Monotheisms*. Translated by W. Hoban. Cambridge: Polity Press.

Smith, C. (2011). *Lost in Transition. The Dark Side of Emerging Adulthood*. Oxford: Oxford University Press.

Smith, J. K. A. (2006). *Who's Afraid of Postmodernism? Taking Derrida, Lyotard, and Foucault to Church*. Grand Rapids: Baker Academic.

Smith, J. K. A. (2014a). *Who's Afraid of Relativism? Community, Contingency, and Creaturehood*. Grand Rapids: Baker Academic.

Smith, J. K. A. (2014b). Echeverria's Protestant Epistemology: A Catholic Response. *Calvin Theological Journal*, 49, 283–292.

Soskice, J. (2023). *Naming God: Addressing the Divine in Philosophy, Theology and Scripture*. Cambridge: Cambridge University Press.

Swoyer, C. (2010). Relativism. In *The Stanford Encyclopedia of Philosophy*. Spring 2010 Edition, https://plato.stanford.edu/archIves/spr2010/entries/relativism/#2.

Tahko, T. E. & Lowe, J. E. (2020). Onotological Dependence. In *The Stanford Encyclopedia of Philosophy*, https://plato.stanford.edu/entries/dependence-ontological.

Trigg, R. (1983). Religion and the Threat of Relativism. *Religious Studies*, 19, 297–310.

Trigg, R. (2001). *Understanding Social Science. A Philosophical Introduction to Social Sciences*. 2nd ed. Oxford: Oxford University Press.

Trigg, R. (2020). *Monotheism and Religious Diversity*. Cambridge: Cambridge University Press.

Vanhoozer, K. J., ed. (2003). *The Cambridge Companion to Postmodern Theology*. Cambridge: Cambridge University Press.

Vattimo, G. (2011). *A Farewell to Truth*. Translated by W. McCuaig. New York: Columbia University Press.

Verhey, A. (2012). The Gospels and Christian Ethics. In R. Gill, ed., *The Cambridge Companion to Christian Ethics*. 2nd ed. Cambridge: Cambridge University Press, 41–53.

Wahlberg, M. (2020). Divine Revelation. In *The Stanford Encyclopedia of Philosophy*, https://plato.stanford.edu/entries/divine-revelation/index.html.

Waines, D. (2003). *An Introduction to Islam*. 2nd ed. Cambridge: Cambridge University Press.

Ward, K. (2011). Religion and Revelation. In C. Meister, ed., *The Oxford Handbook of Religious Diversity*. Oxford: Oxford University Press, 169–182.

Webb, M. O. (2023). Jain Philosophy. In *The Internet Encyclopedia of Philosophy*, https://iep.utm.edu/jain.

Westacott, E. (2024). Moral Relativism. In *The Internet Encyclopedia of Philosophy*, https://iep.utm.edu/moral-re.

Wilfred, F. (2006). In Praise of Christian Relativism. In E. Borgman & M. Junker-Kenny, eds., *The New Pontificate: A Time for Change?* Concilium, 42 (1). London: SCM Press, 86–94.

Williamson, T. (2005). Knowledge, Context, and the Agent's Point of View. In G. Preyer & G. Peter, eds., *Contextualism in Philosophy: Knowledge, Meaning, and Truth*. Oxford: Oxford University Press, 91–114.

Wright, C. (2010). Intuitionism, Realism, Relativism, and Rhubarb. In M. Krausz, ed., *Relativism: A Contemporary Anthology*. New York: Columbia University Press, 330–355.

Acknowledgements

I would like to thank the editors of this Cambridge Elements series, Chad Meister and Paul Moser, for their support of my book project. I am also grateful to two anonymous reviewers for their helpful comments on the manuscript. Special thanks go to Anthony Bowen, Paul Dominiak, Lukas Klimke, Aaron Langenfeld, Roy Pinkerton, Heather Rendell, and Sandra Scholz.

This Element was written during a research semester supported by scholarships at Harvard Divinity School and Jesus College, Cambridge. In this regard, I would like to thank especially Francis C. Clooney, S.J., Janet M. Soskice, and Ian Wilson.

Cambridge Elements ≡

Religion and Monotheism

Paul K. Moser

Loyola University Chicago

Paul K. Moser is Professor of Philosophy at Loyola University Chicago. He is the author of *God in Moral Experience; Paul's Gospel of Divine Self-Sacrifice; The Divine Goodness of Jesus; Divine Guidance; Understanding Religious Experience; The God Relationship; The Elusive God* (winner of national book award from the Jesuit Honor Society); *The Evidence for God; The Severity of God; Knowledge and Evidence* (all Cambridge University Press); and *Philosophy after Objectivity* (Oxford University Press); coauthor of *Theory of Knowledge* (Oxford University Press); editor of *Jesus and Philosophy* (Cambridge University Press) and *The Oxford Handbook of Epistemology* (Oxford University Press); and coeditor of *The Wisdom of the Christian Faith* (Cambridge University Press). He is the coeditor with Chad Meister of the book series *Cambridge Studies in Religion, Philosophy, and Society.*

Chad Meister

Affiliate Scholar, Ansari Institute for Global Engagement with Religion, University of Notre Dame

Chad Meister is Affiliate Scholar at the Ansari Institute for Global Engagement with Religion at the University of Notre Dame. His authored and co-authored books include *Evil: A Guide for the Perplexed* (Bloomsbury Academic, 2nd edition); *Introducing Philosophy of Religion* (Routledge); *Introducing Christian Thought* (Routledge, 2nd edition); and *Contemporary Philosophical Theology* (Routledge). He has edited or co-edited the following: *The Oxford Handbook of Religious Diversity* (Oxford University Press); *Debating Christian Theism* (Oxford University Press); with Paul Moser, *The Cambridge Companion to the Problem of Evil* (Cambridge University Press); and with Charles Taliaferro, *The History of Evil* (Routledge, in six volumes). He is the co-editor with Paul Moser of the book series *Cambridge Studies in Religion, Philosophy, and Society.*

About the Series

This Cambridge Element series publishes original concise volumes on monotheism and its significance. Monotheism has occupied inquirers since the time of the Biblical patriarch, and it continues to attract interdisciplinary academic work today. Engaging, current, and concise, the Elements benefit teachers, researched, and advanced students in religious studies, Biblical studies, theology, philosophy of religion, and related fields.

Cambridge Elements ☰

Religion and Monotheism

Elements in the Series